FOR ORGANS, PIANOS & ELECTRONIC KEYBOARDS

SACRED SOUNDS

22

E-Z does it! That's why E-Z Play TODAY Music was created. This series has been designed with a special music notation for instant playing enjoyment.

The collection of songs in each book has been specifically arranged for use with all major brand organs, including chord organs and those with automatic chord units. Special chord notation is also included for the triad and conventional chord player. The entire series provides a play-on-sight repertoire filled with musical fun for everyone . . . delightful tunes that will appeal to every musical interest.

Contents

2 Abide With Me
4 All Hail The Power Of Jesus' Name
6 Blessed Assurance
8 Blest Be The Tie That Binds
10 Church's One Foundation, The
12 Cleanse Me
14 Crown Him With Many Crowns
16 Fairest Lord Jesus
18 Faith Of Our Fathers
20 Give Me That Old Time Religion
22 In The Garden
24 In The Sweet Bye and Bye
28 Jesus, Lover Of My Soul
30 Joshua Fit The Battle Of Jericho
27 Lord Is My Shepherd, The
32 Nearer, My God, To Thee

34 O God, Our Help In Ages Past
36 O Worship The King
38 Old Rugged Cross, The
40 Onward, Christian Soldiers
42 Pass Me Not, O Gentle Saviour
64 Praise God From Whom All Blessings Flow
44 Rock Of Ages
46 Saviour, Like A Shepherd Lead Us
48 Shall We Gather At The River?
50 Softly And Tenderly
52 Sweet Hour Of Prayer
54 Swing Low, Sweet Chariot
56 We Gather Together To Ask The Lord's Blessing
58 Were You There?
60 What A Friend We Have In Jesus
62 Whispering Hope

ISBN 0-7935-0533-X

7777 W. BLUEMOUND RD. P.O. BOX 13819 MILWAUKEE, WI 53213

E-Z Play ® TODAY Music Notation © 1975 HAL LEONARD PUBLISHING CORPORATION
Copyright © 1991 HAL LEONARD PUBLISHING CORPORATION
International Copyright Secured   All Rights Reserved

For all works contained herein:
Unauthorized copying, arranging, adapting, recording or public performance is an infringement of copyright.
Infringers are liable under the law.

E-Z PLAY and EASY ELECTRONIC KEYBOARD MUSIC are registered trademarks of HAL LEONARD PUBLISHING CORPORATION

Abide With Me

Registration 3

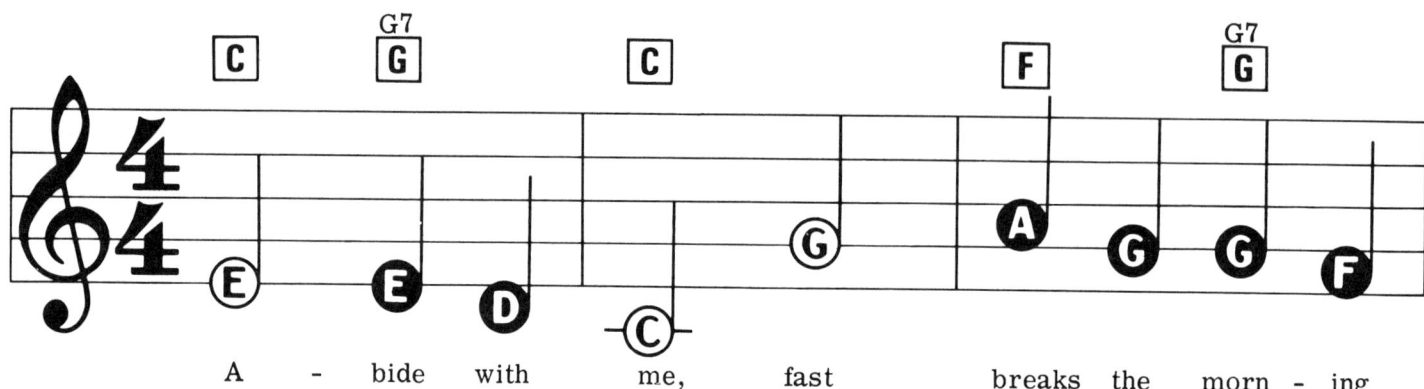
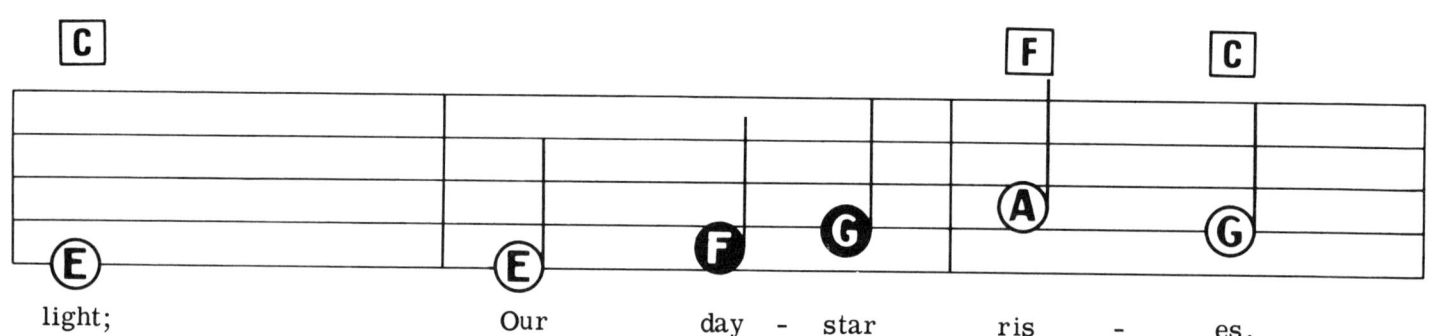
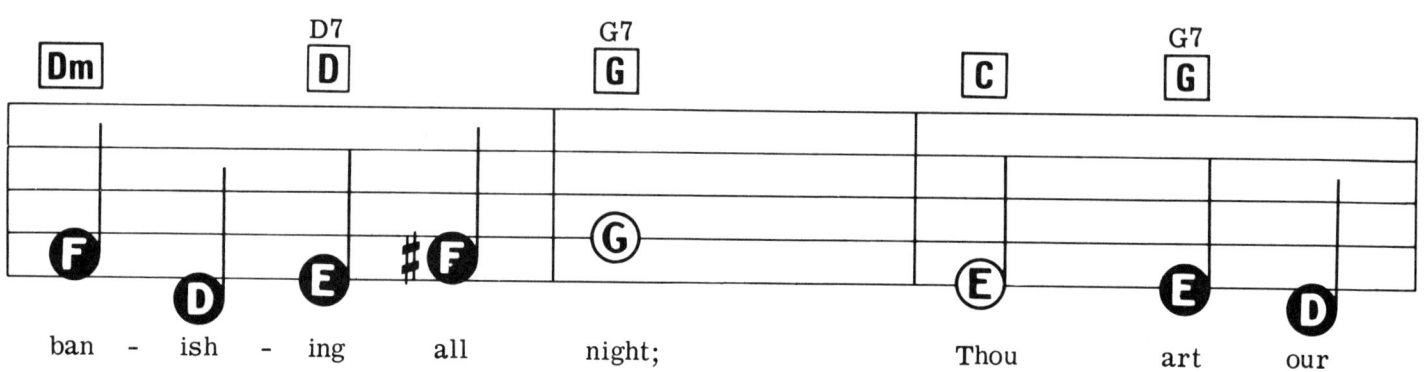
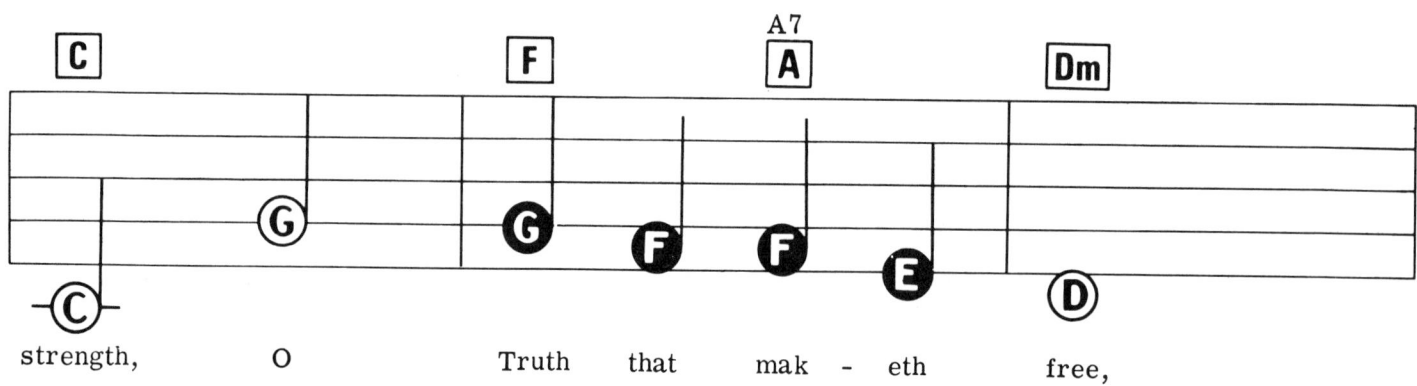

This arr. © Copyright 1975 by HAL LEONARD PUBLISHING CORPORATION, Winona, MN 55987
Made in U.S.A.   International Copyright Secured   All Rights Reserved

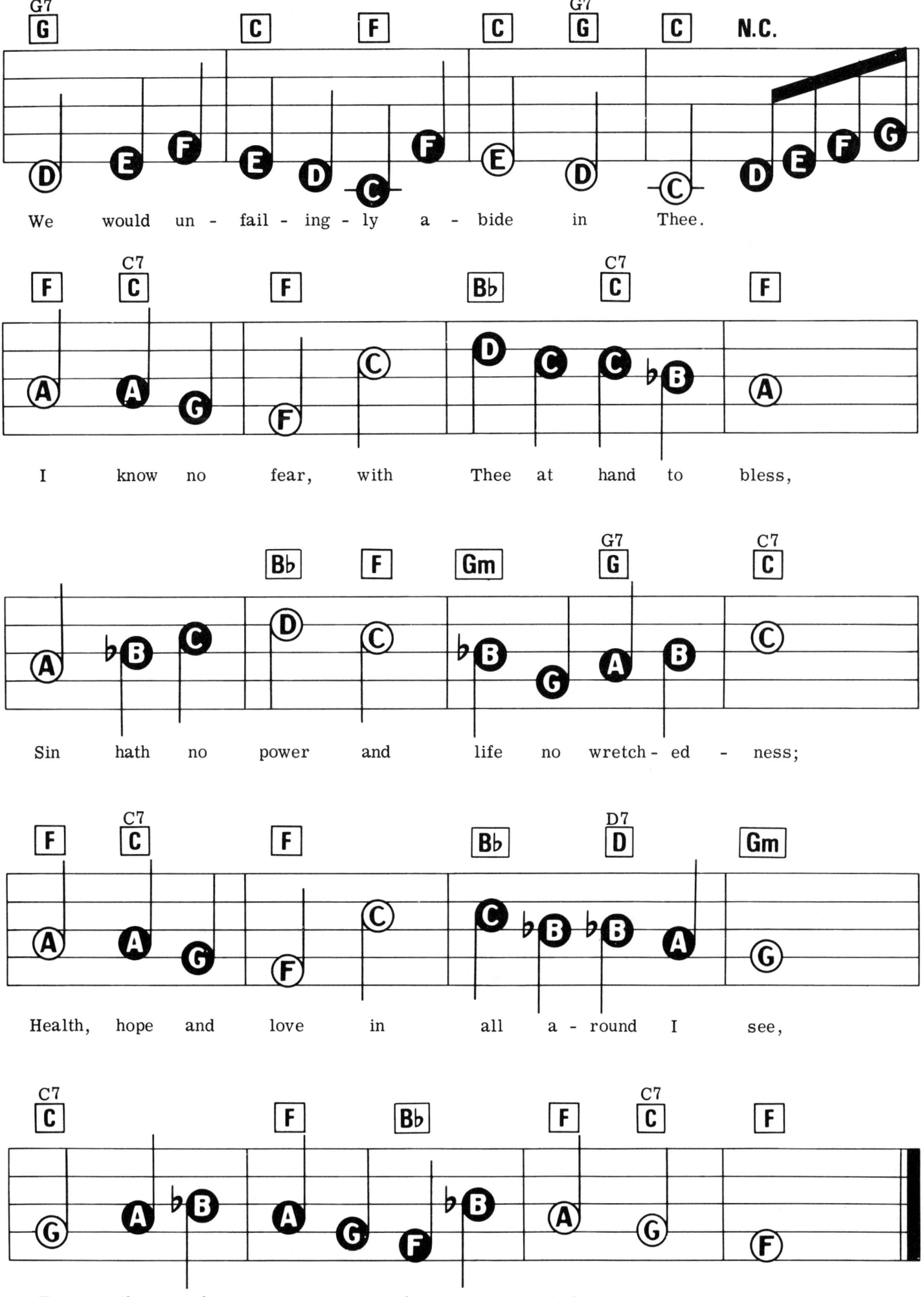

All Hail The Power Of Jesus' Name

Registration 3

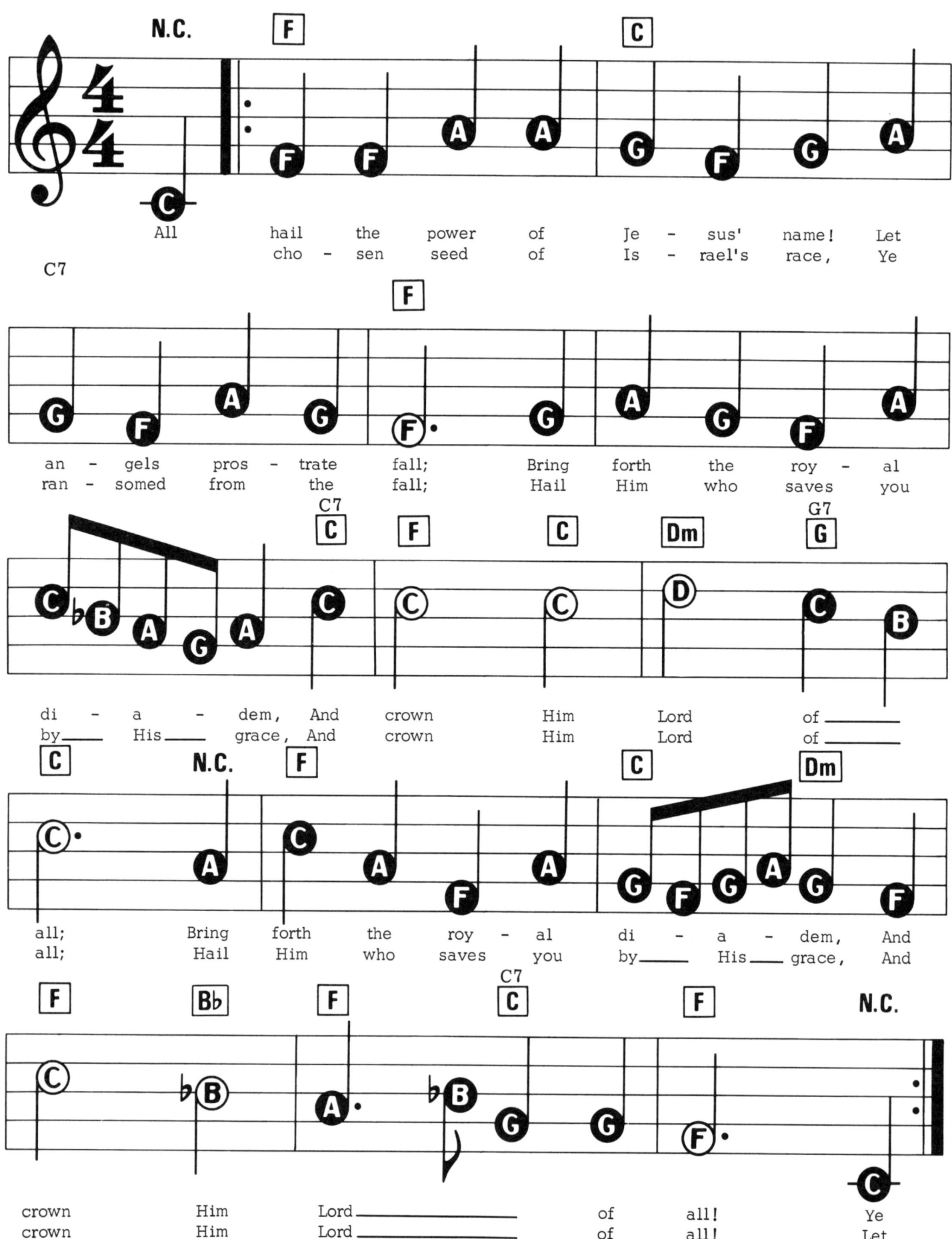

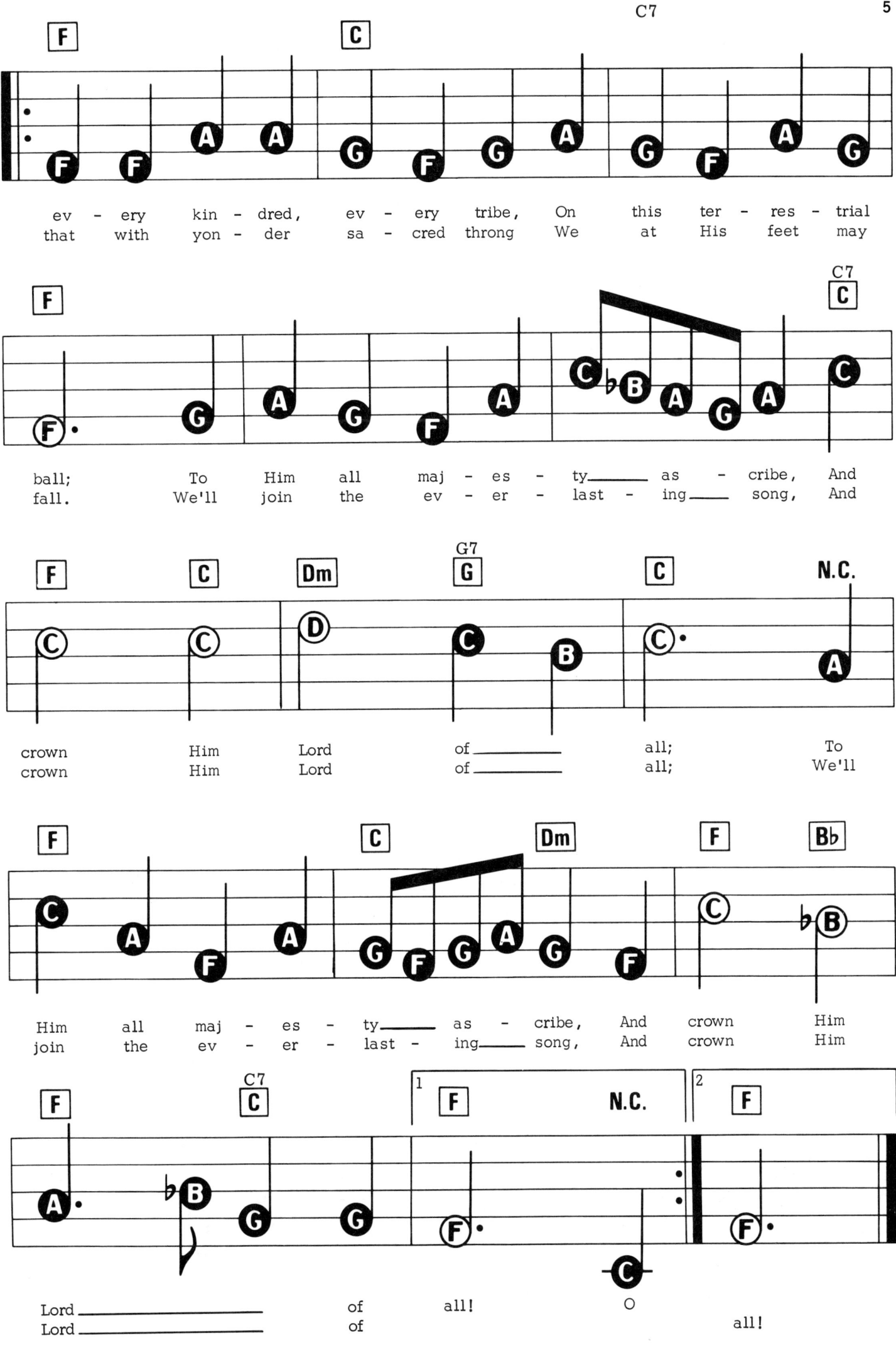

Blessed Assurance

Registration 6
Rhythm: Waltz

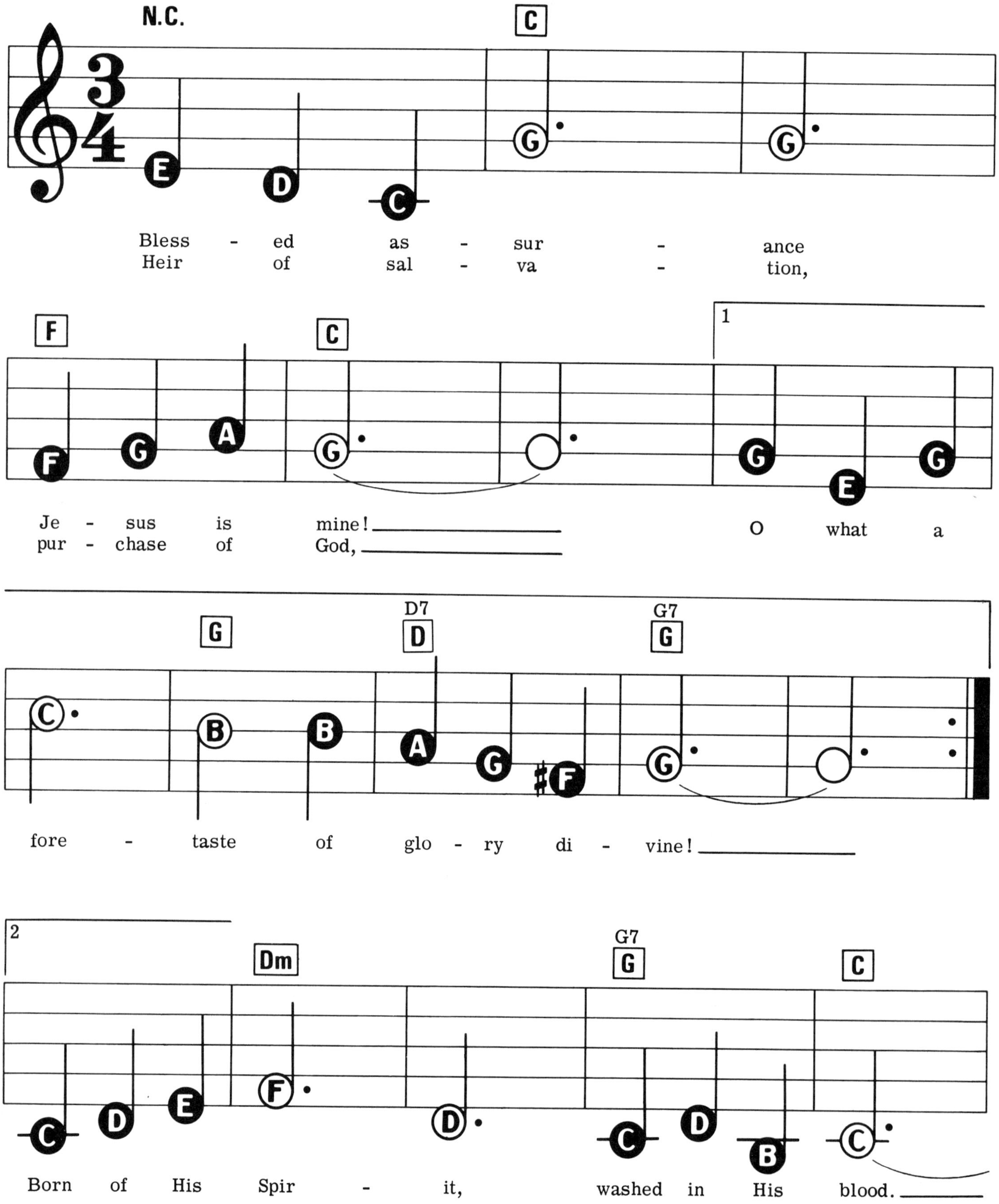

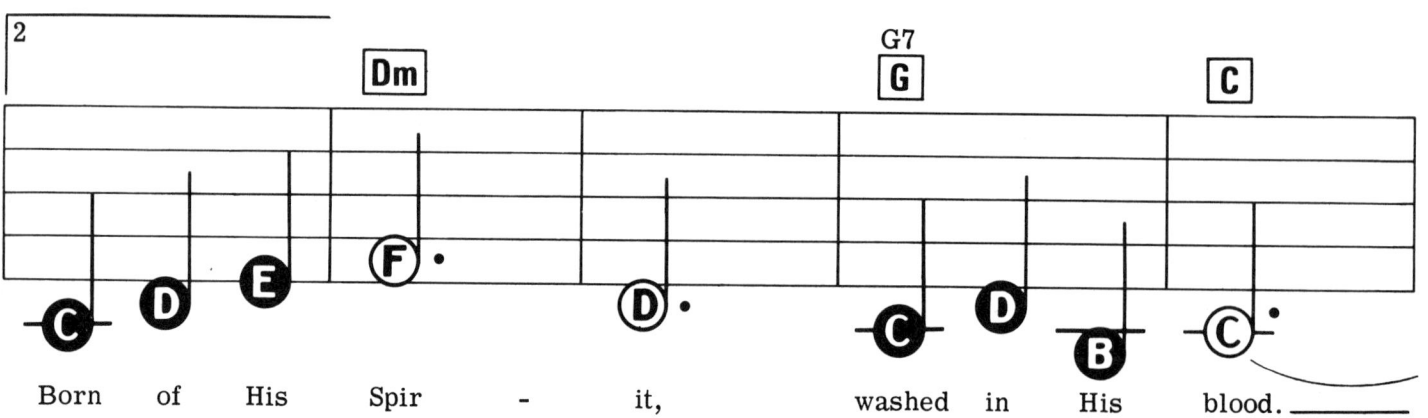

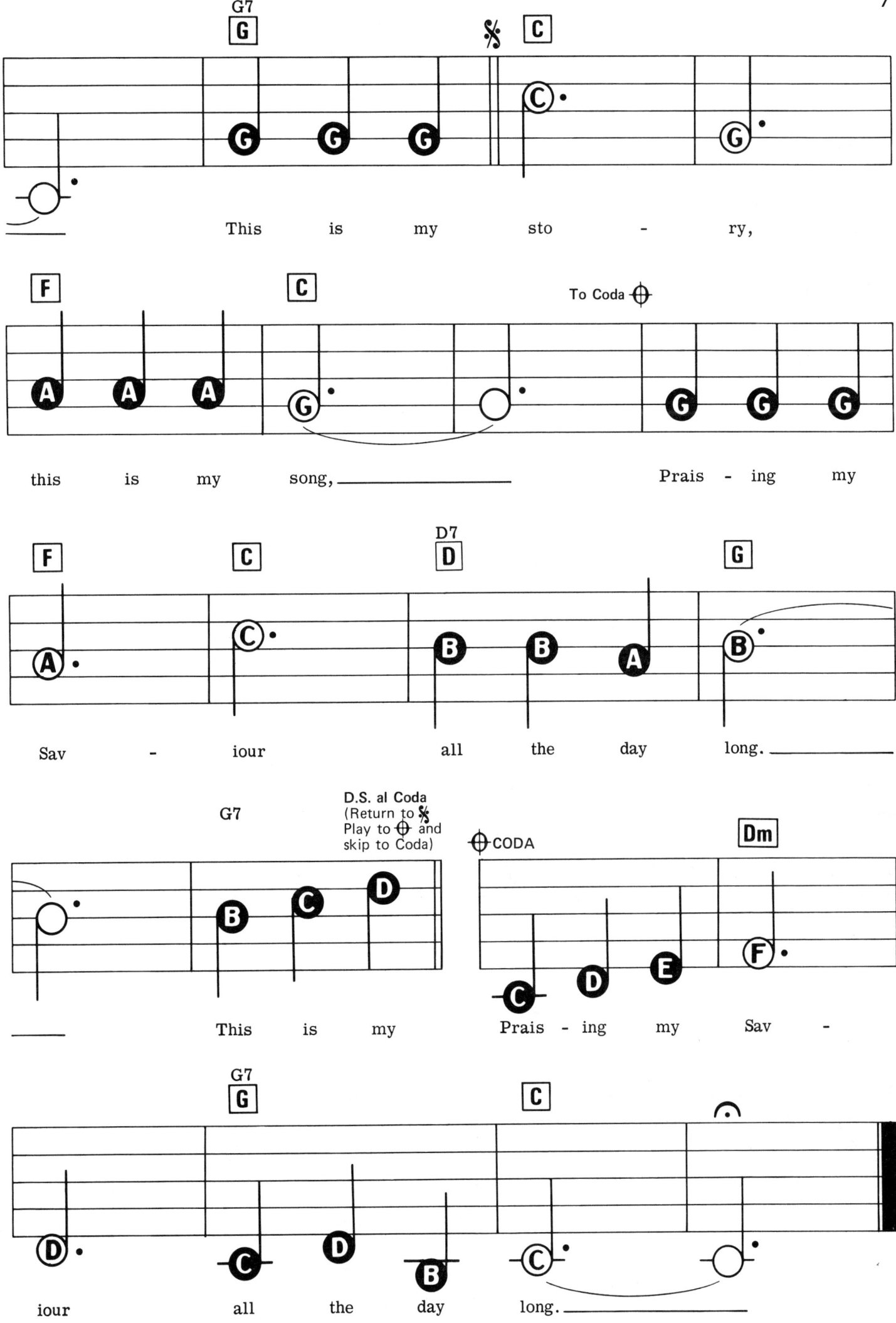

Blest Be The Tie That Binds

Registration 4
Rhythm: Waltz

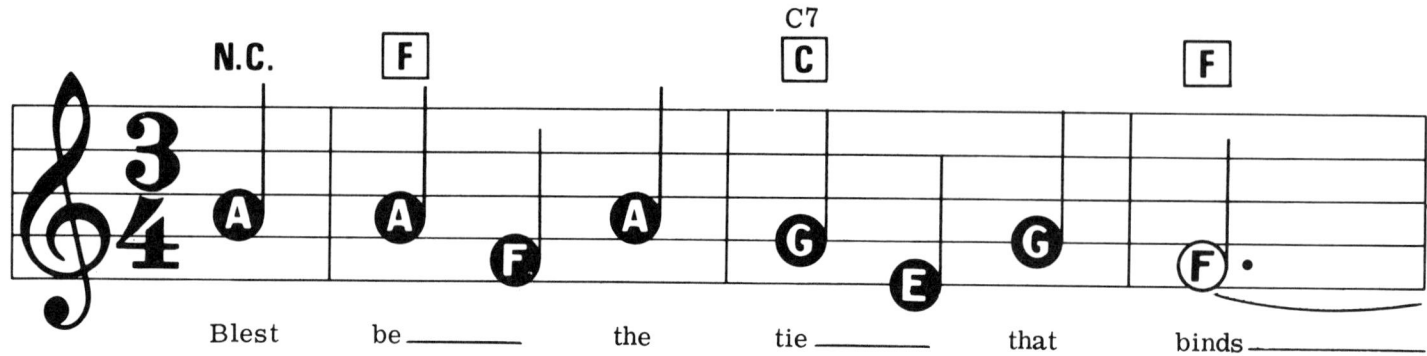

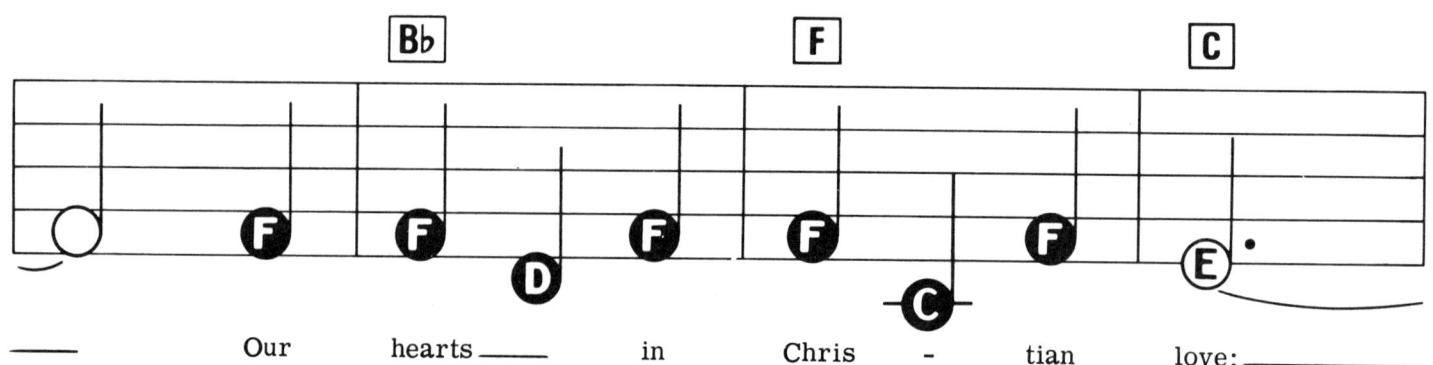

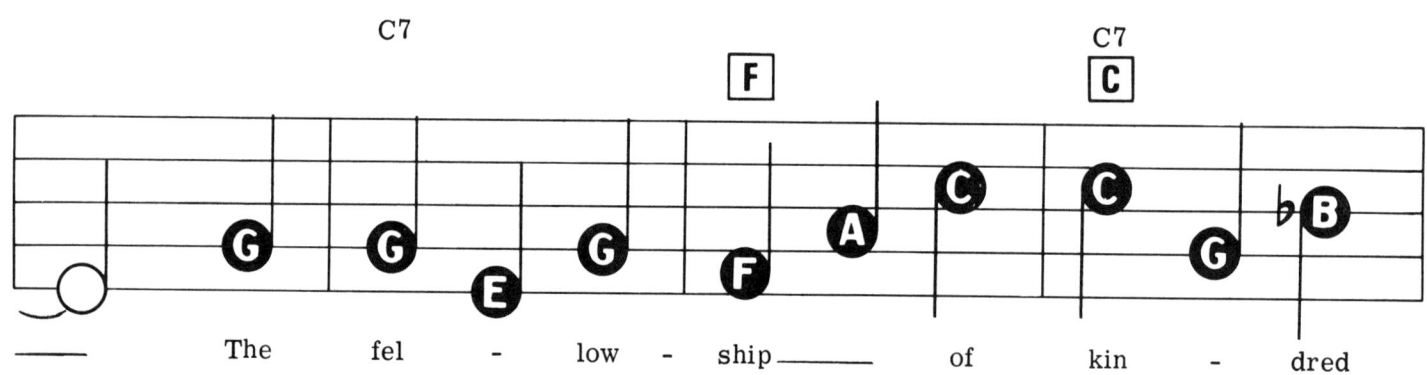

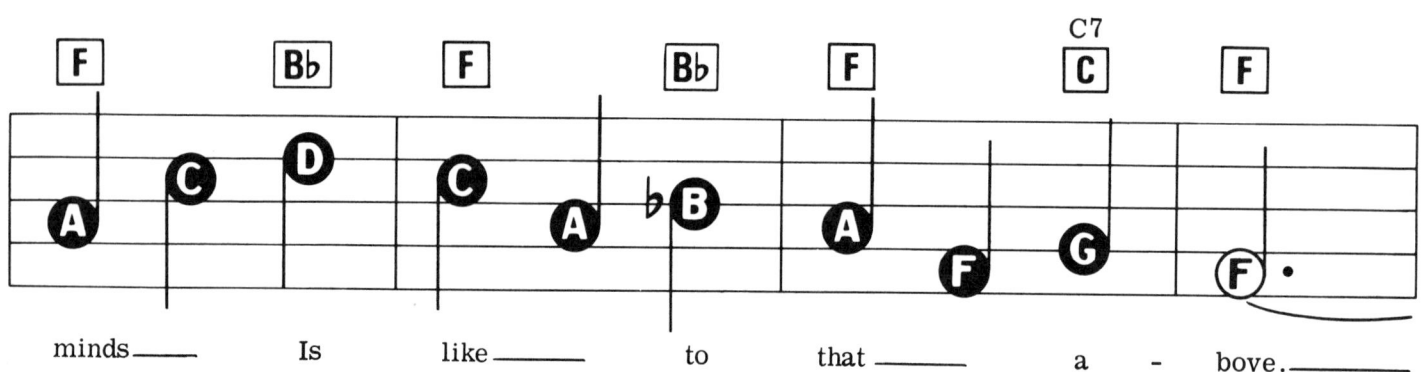

This arr. © Copyright 1975 by HAL LEONARD PUBLISHING CORPORATION, Winona, MN 55987
Made in U.S.A.   International Copyright Secured   All Rights Reserved

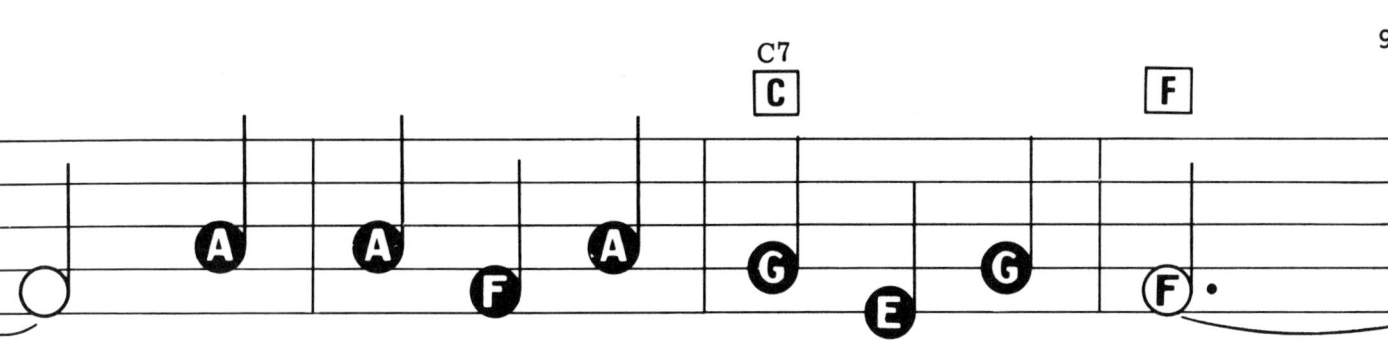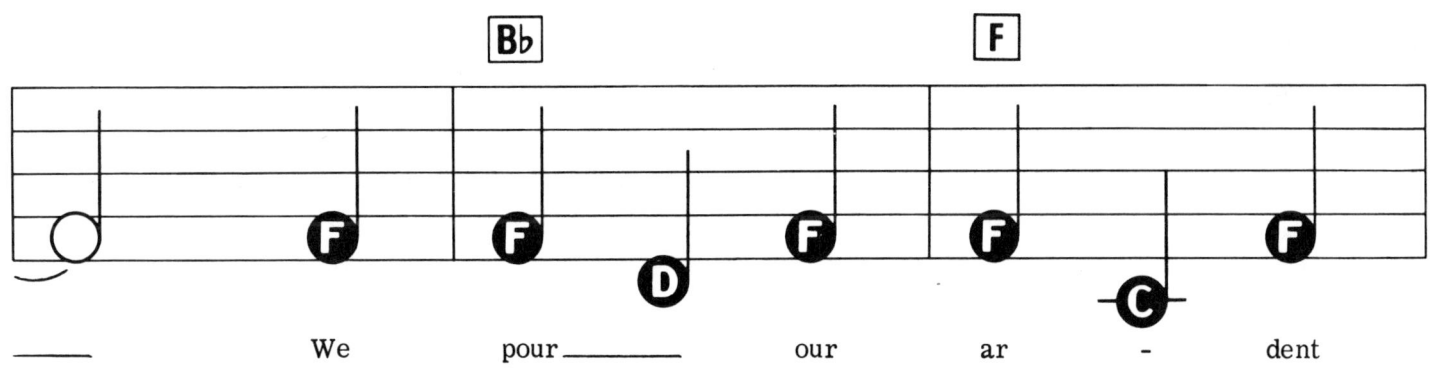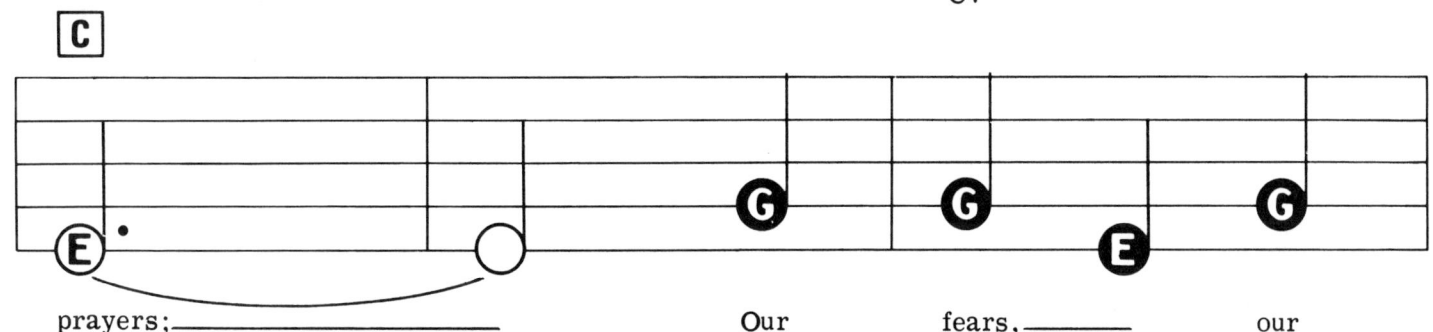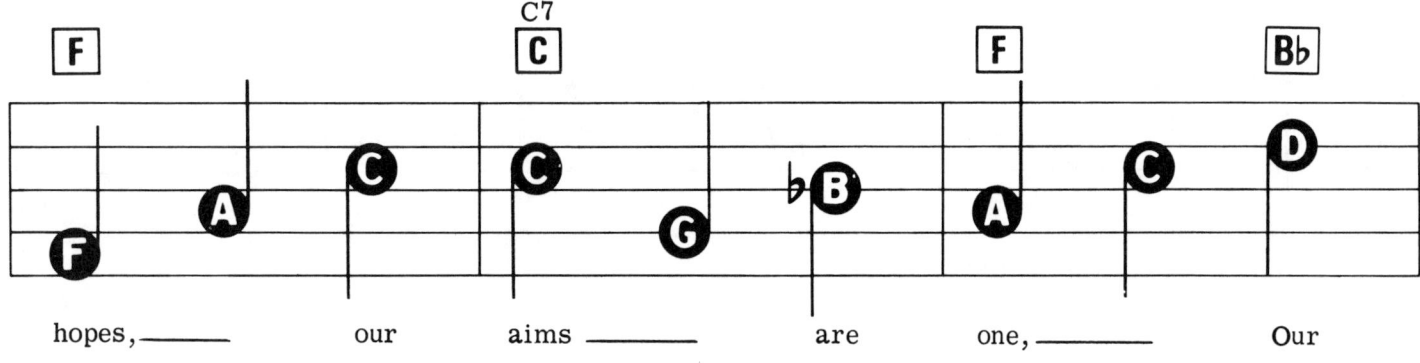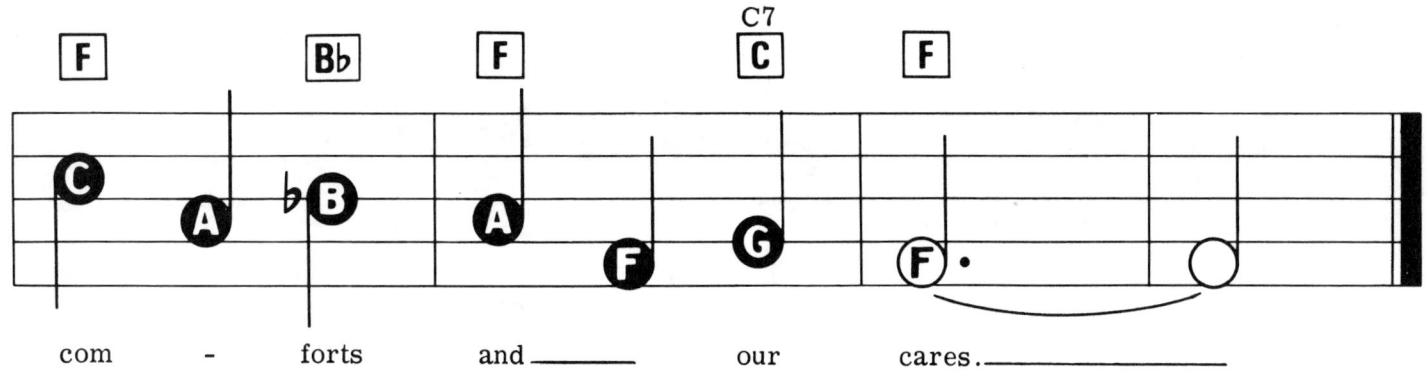

The Church's One Foundation

Registration 2

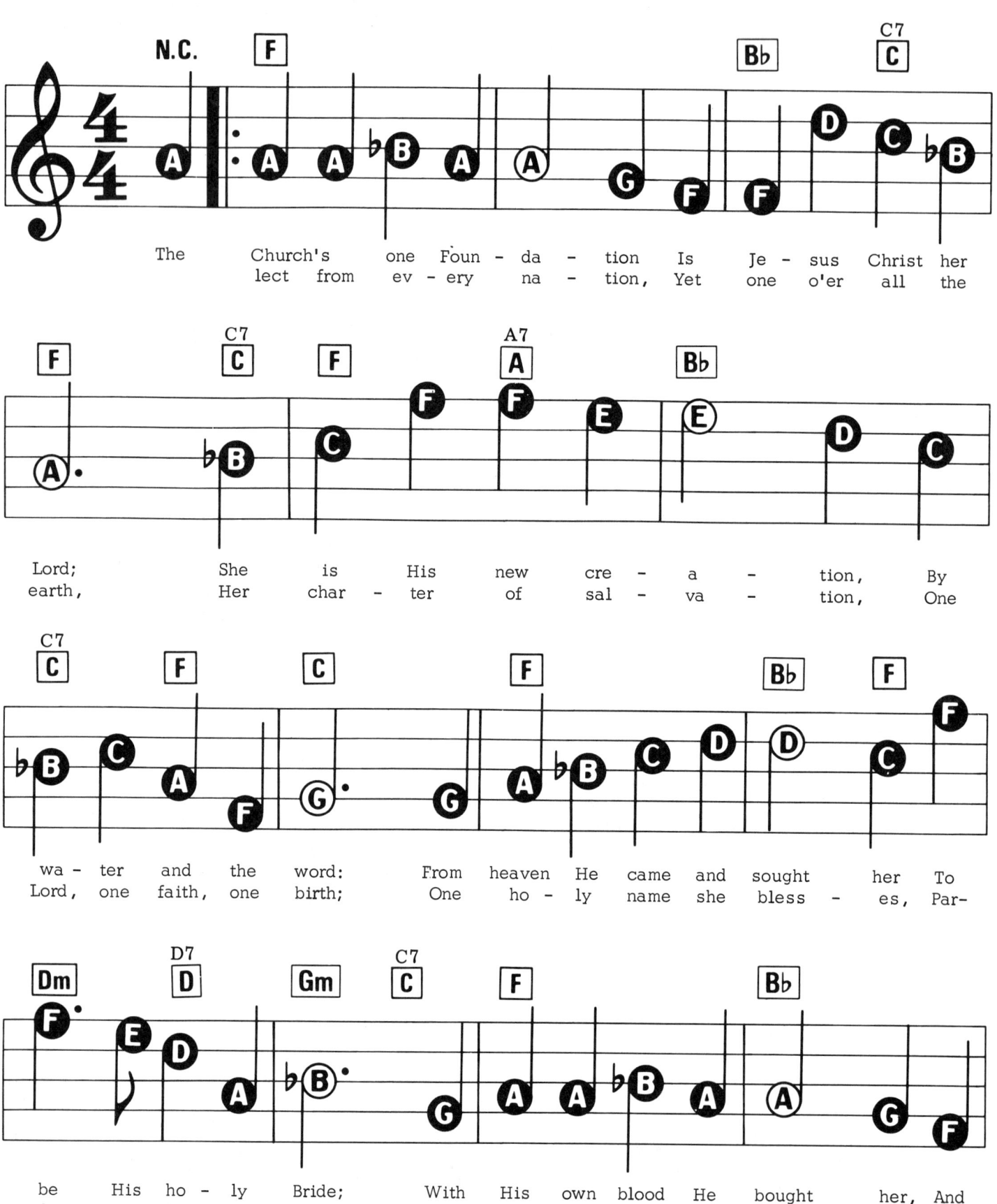

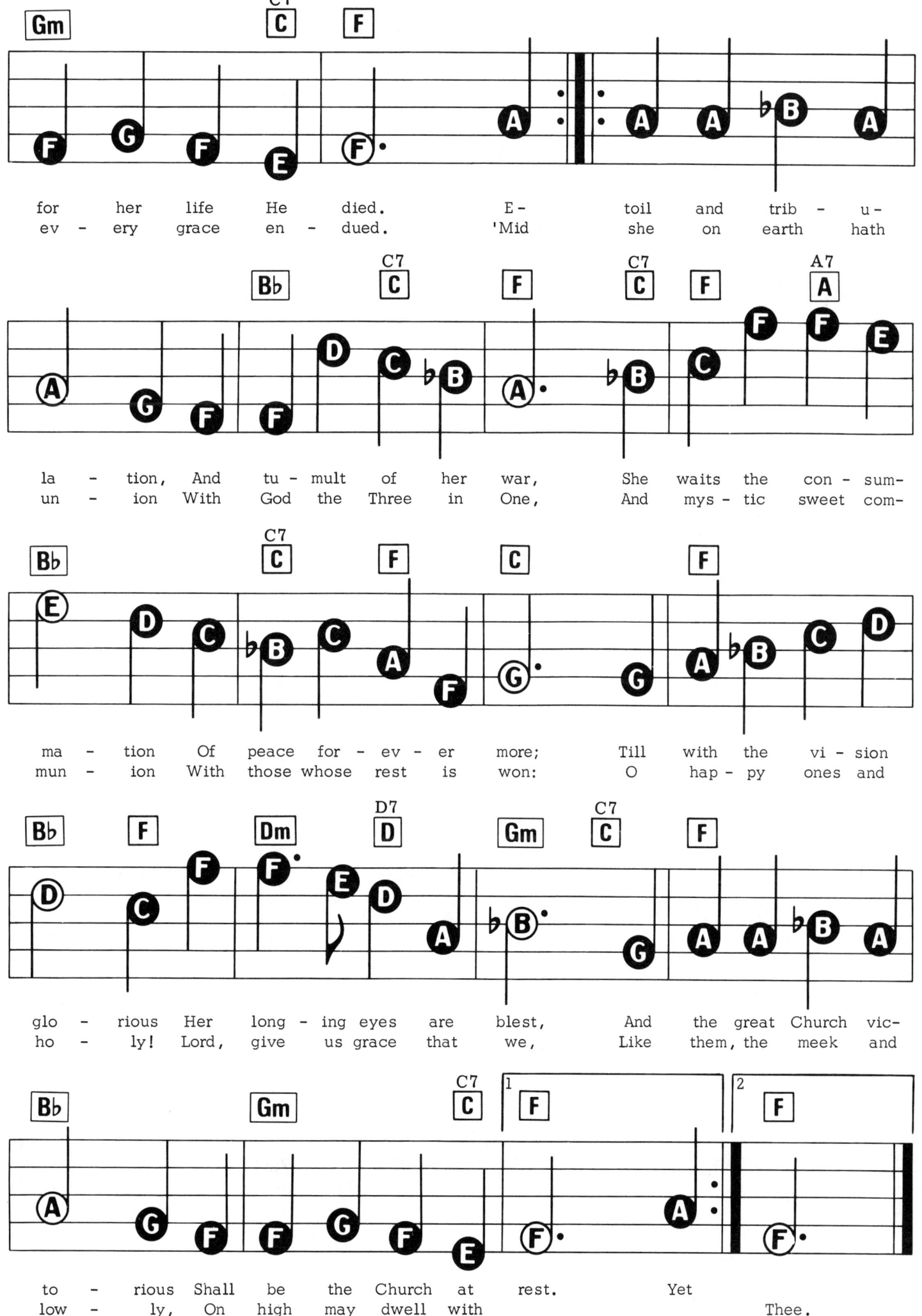

Cleanse Me

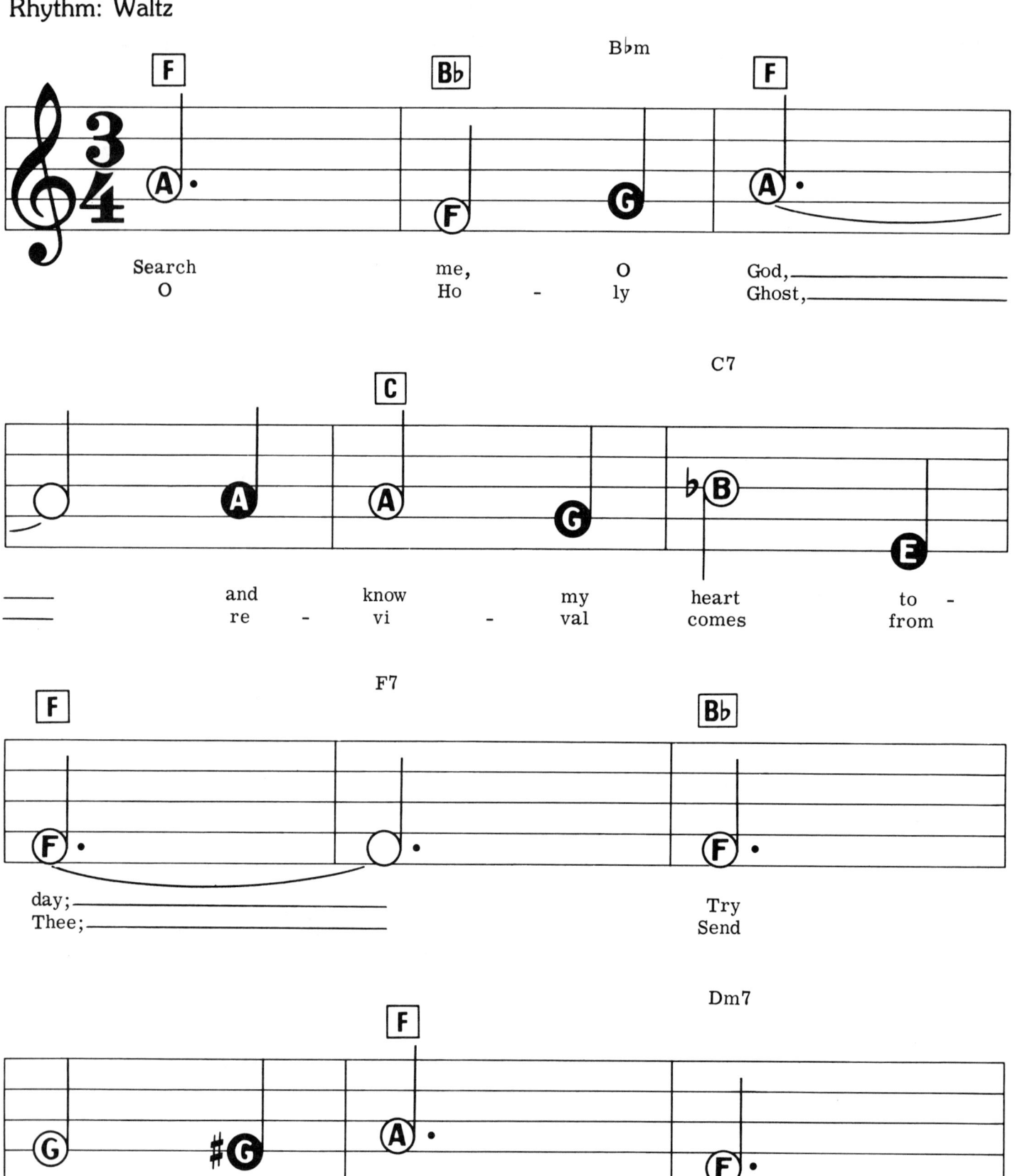

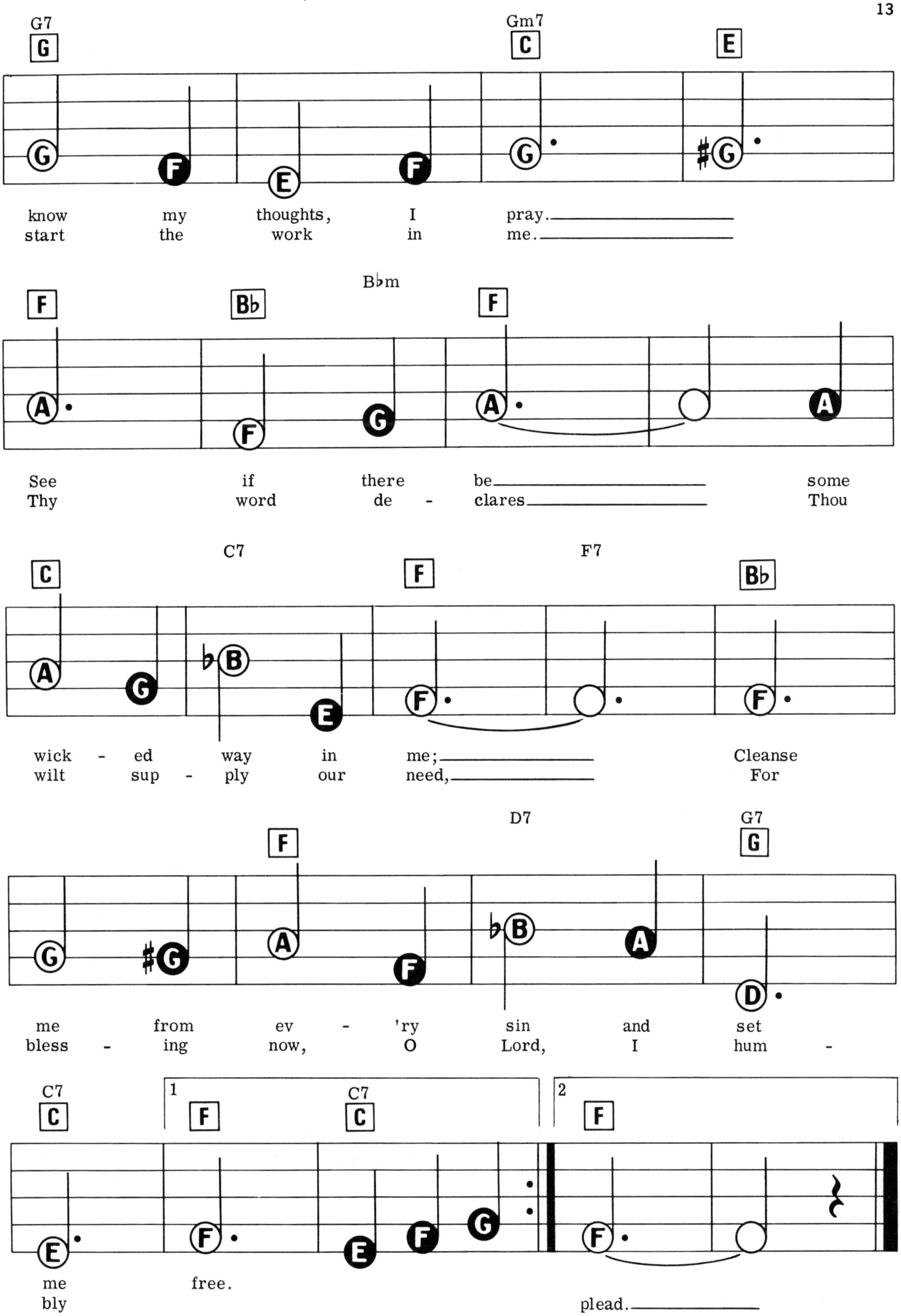
G7 Gm7
know my thoughts, I pray.
start the work in me.
B♭m
See if there be some
Thy word de - clares Thou
C7 F7
wick - ed way in me; Cleanse
wilt sup - ply our need, For
D7 G7
me from ev - 'ry sin and set
bless - ing now, O Lord, I hum -
C7 C7
1 2
me free.
bly plead.

Crown Him With Many Crowns

Registration 2
Rhythm: Waltz

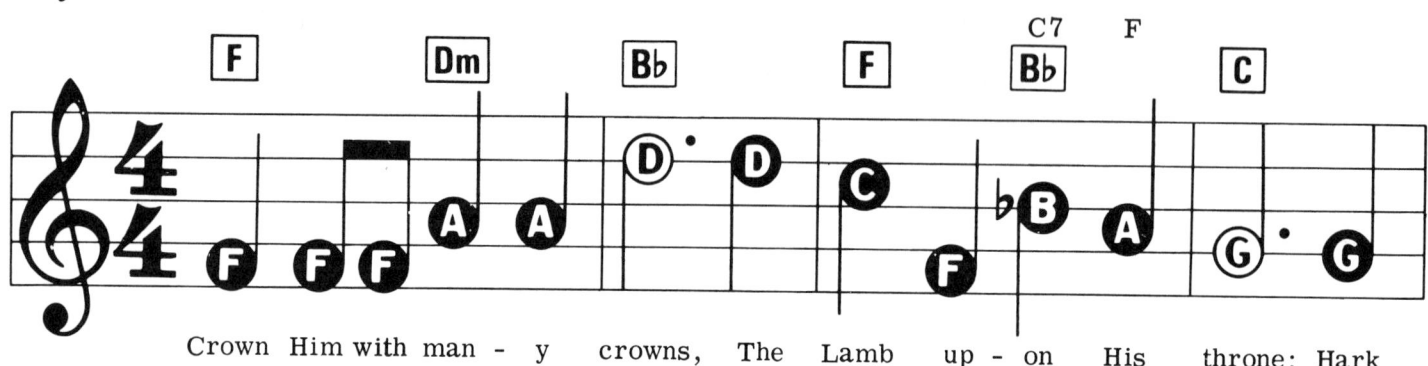

Crown Him with man-y crowns, The Lamb up-on His throne; Hark

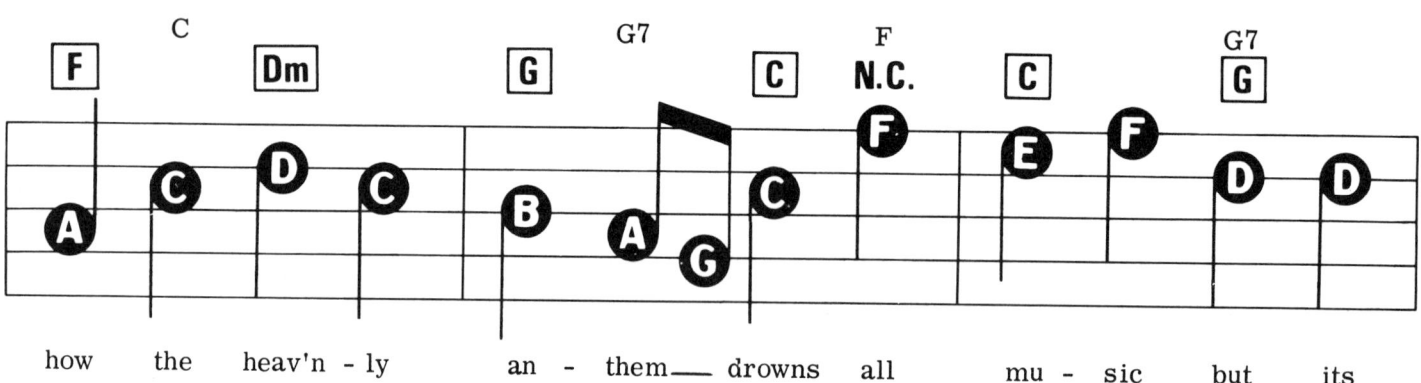

how the heav'n-ly an-them drowns all mu-sic but its

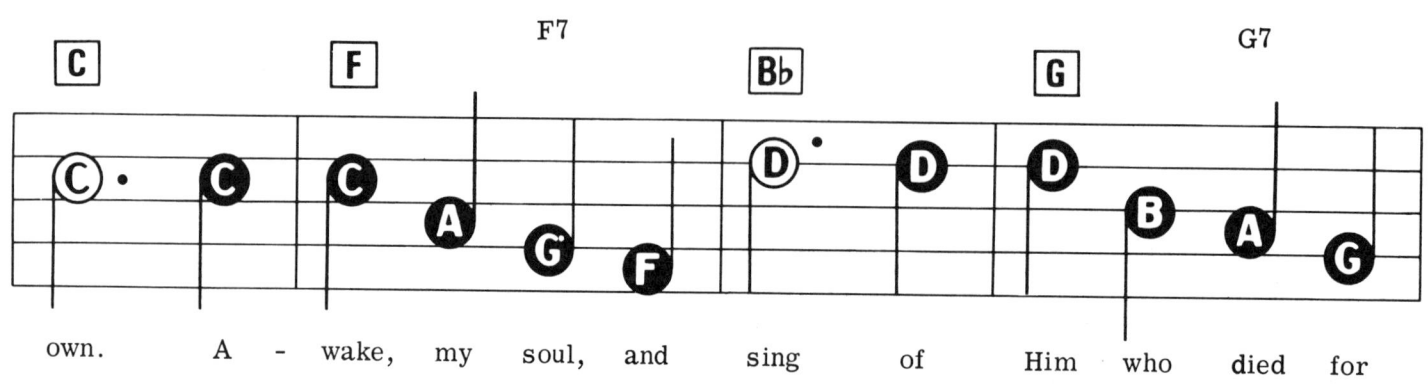

own. A-wake, my soul, and sing of Him who died for

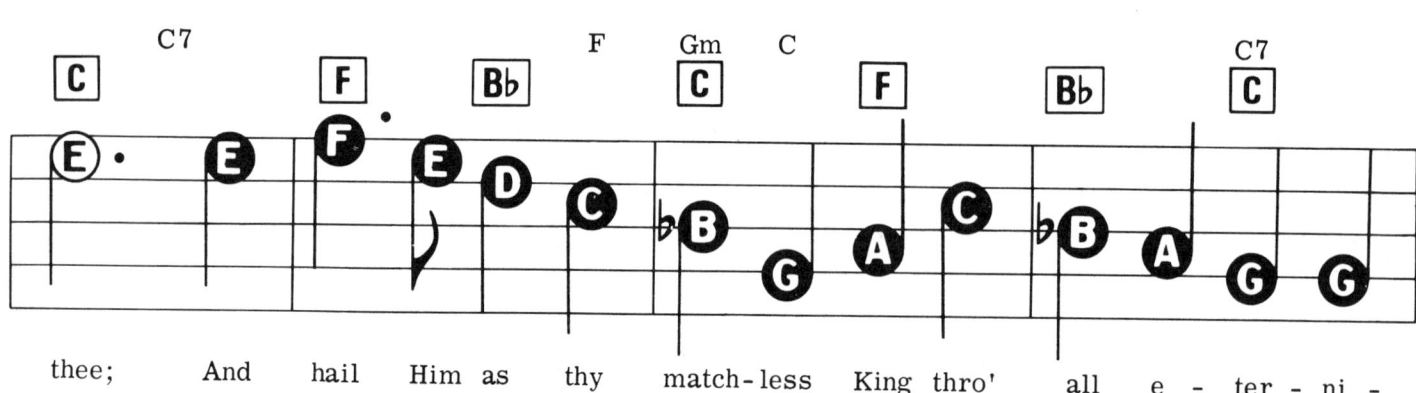

thee; And hail Him as thy match-less King thro' all e-ter-ni-

This arr. © Copyright 1975 by HAL LEONARD PUBLISHING CORPORATION, Winona, MN 55987
Made in U.S.A.　　　International Copyright Secured　　　All Rights Reserved

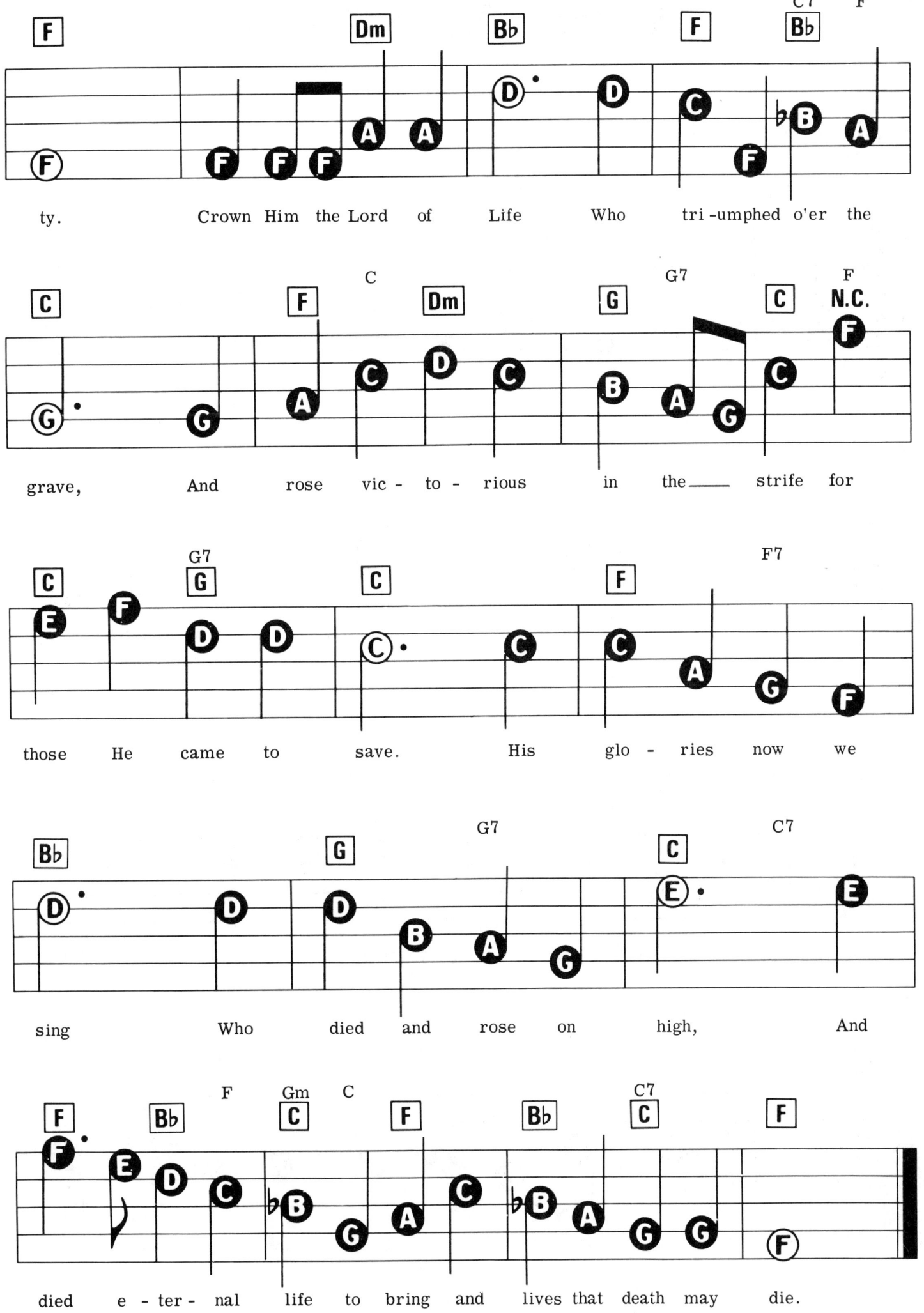

Fairest Lord Jesus

Registration 5

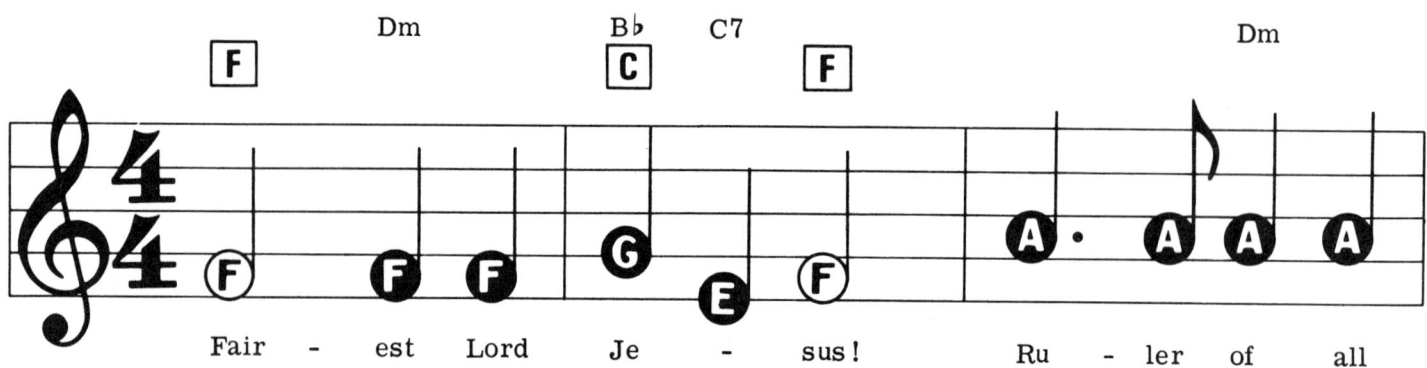
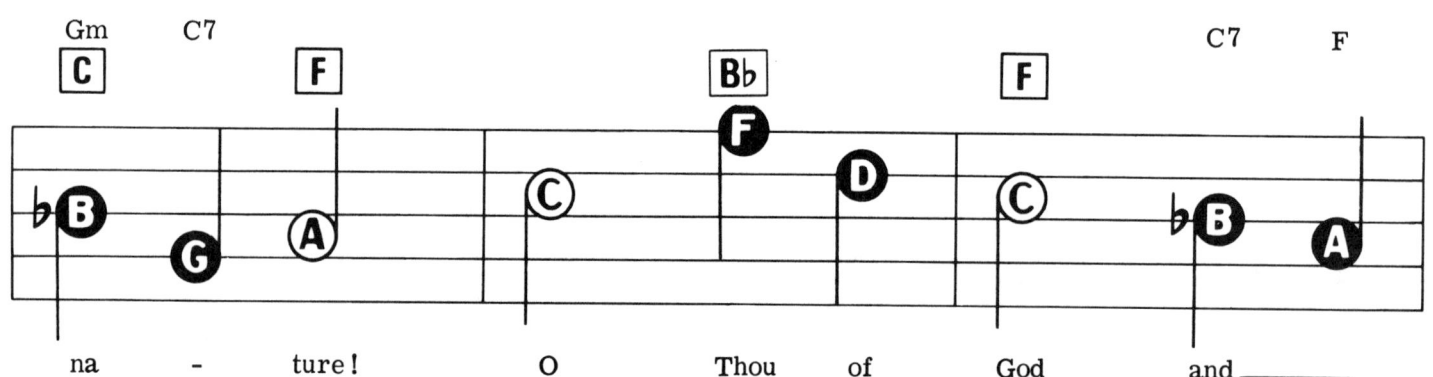
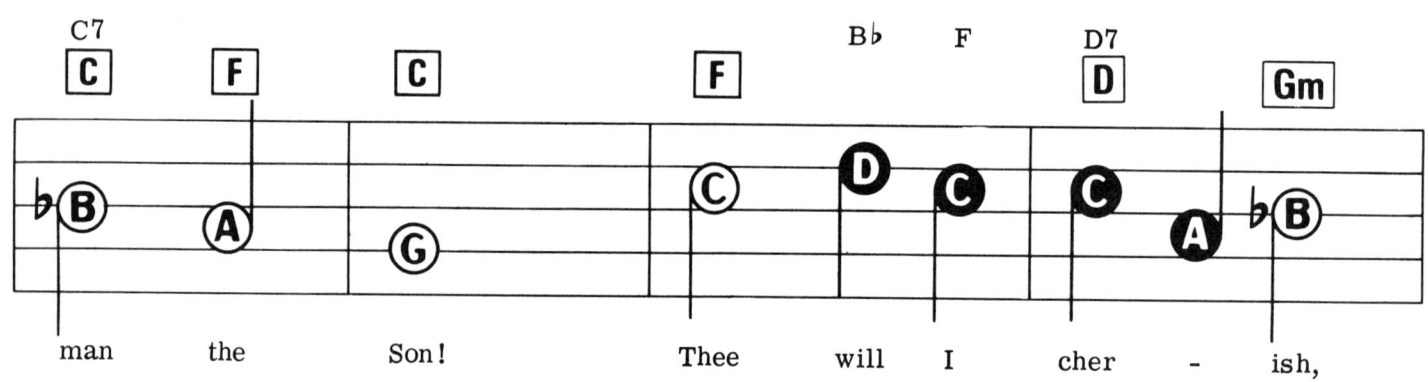
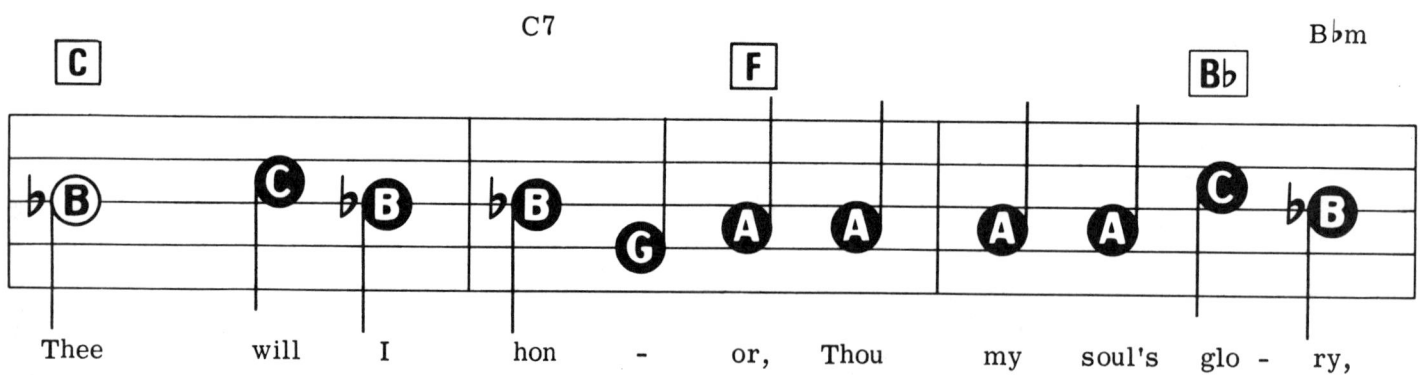

This arr. © Copyright 1975 by HAL LEONARD PUBLISHING CORPORATION, Winona, MN 55987
Made in U.S.A.   International Copyright Secured   All Rights Reserved

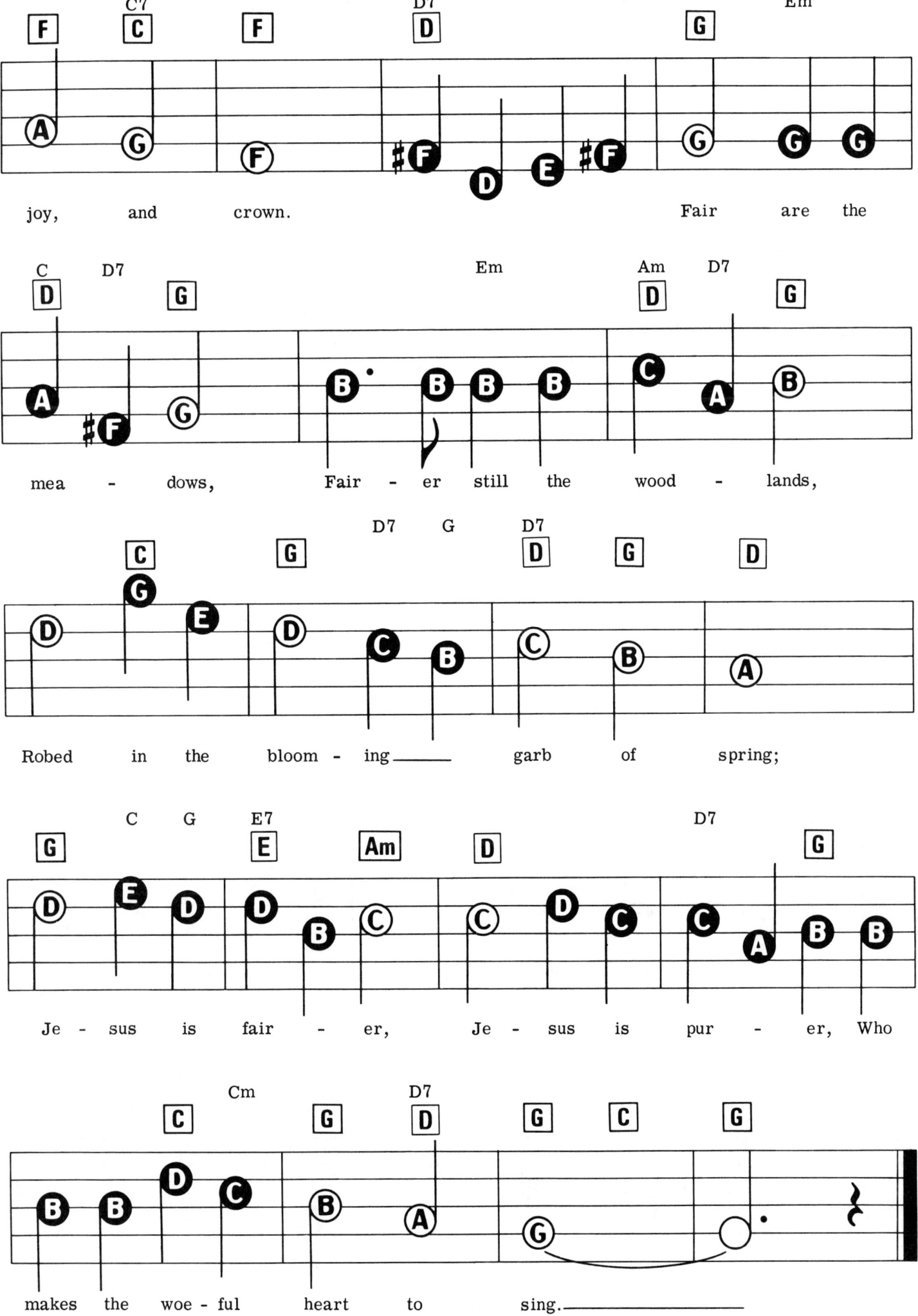

Faith Of Our Fathers

Registration 4
Rhythm: Waltz

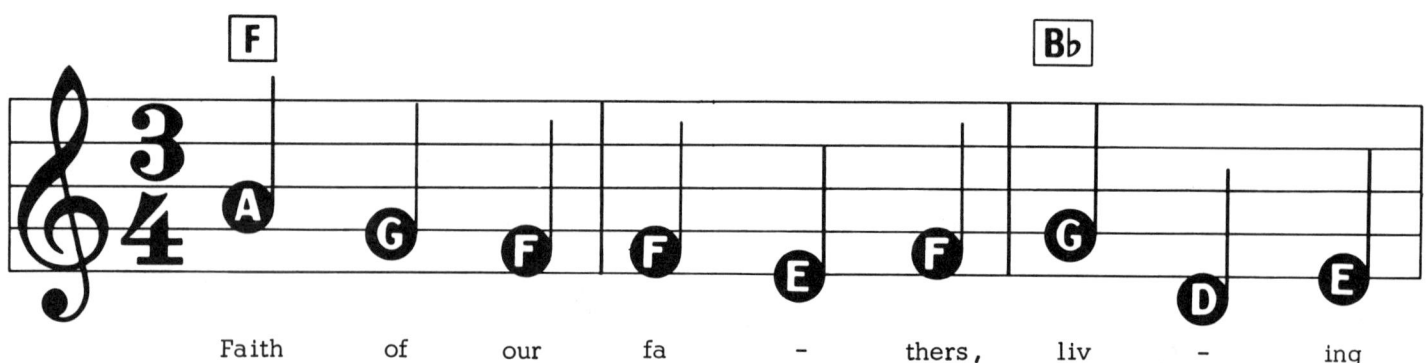

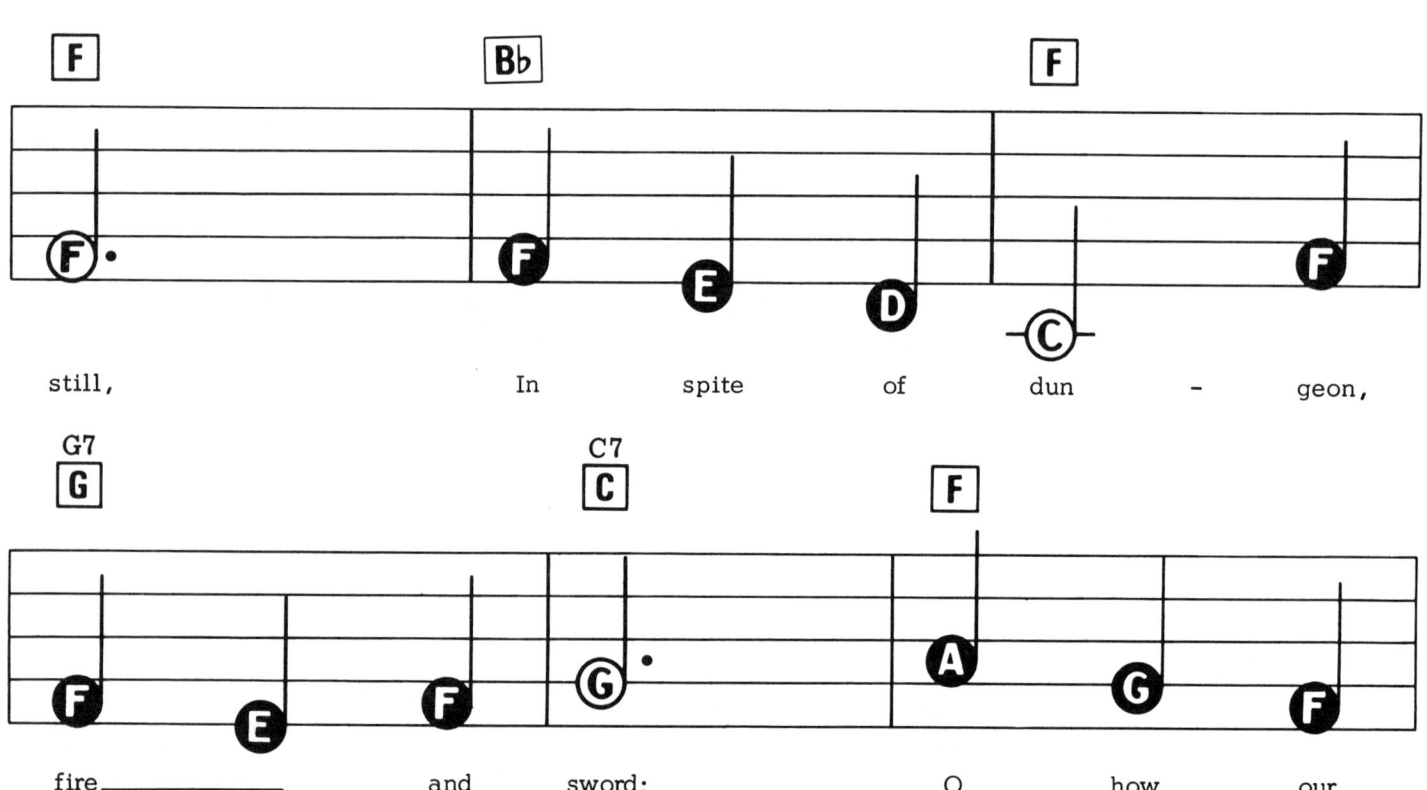

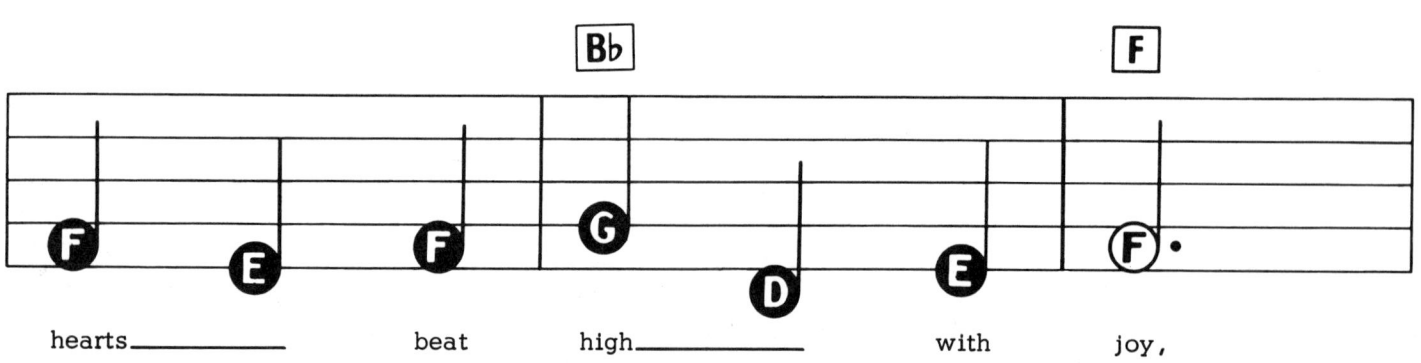

This arrangement © 1977 HAL LEONARD PUBLISHING CORPORATION
Made in U.S.A.   International Copyright Secured   All Rights Reserved

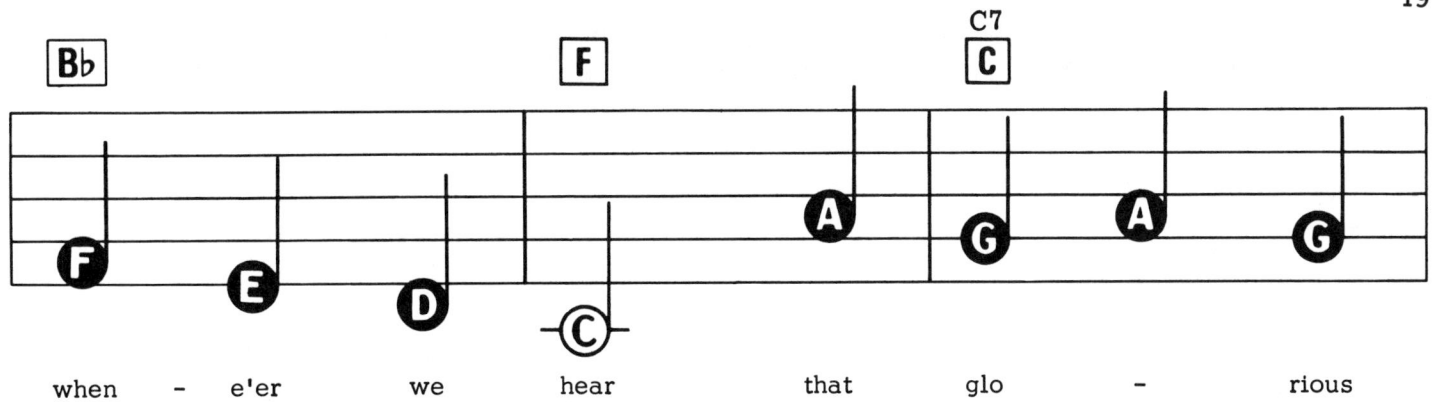
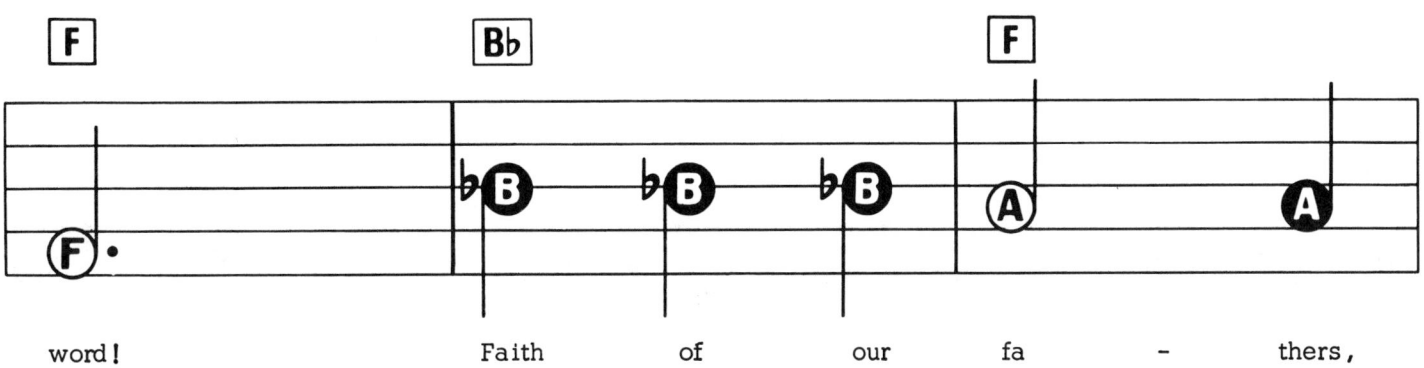
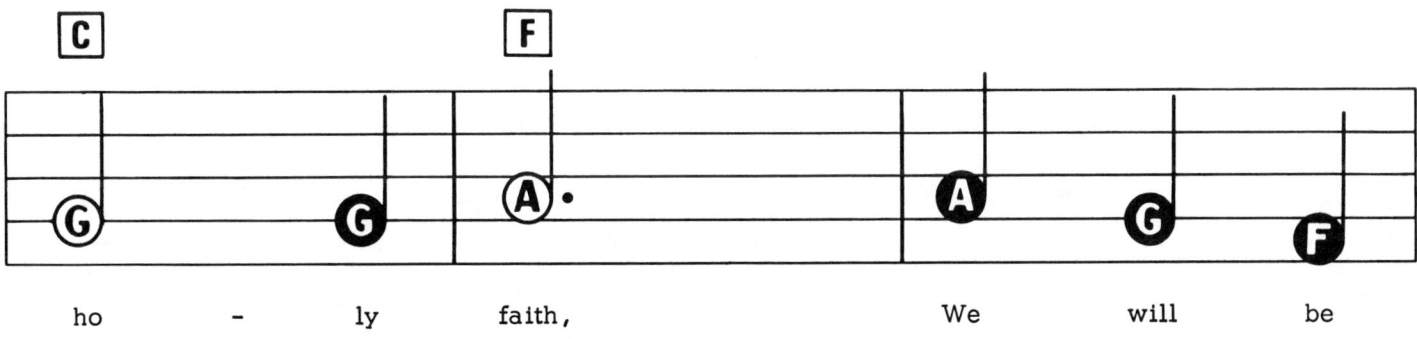
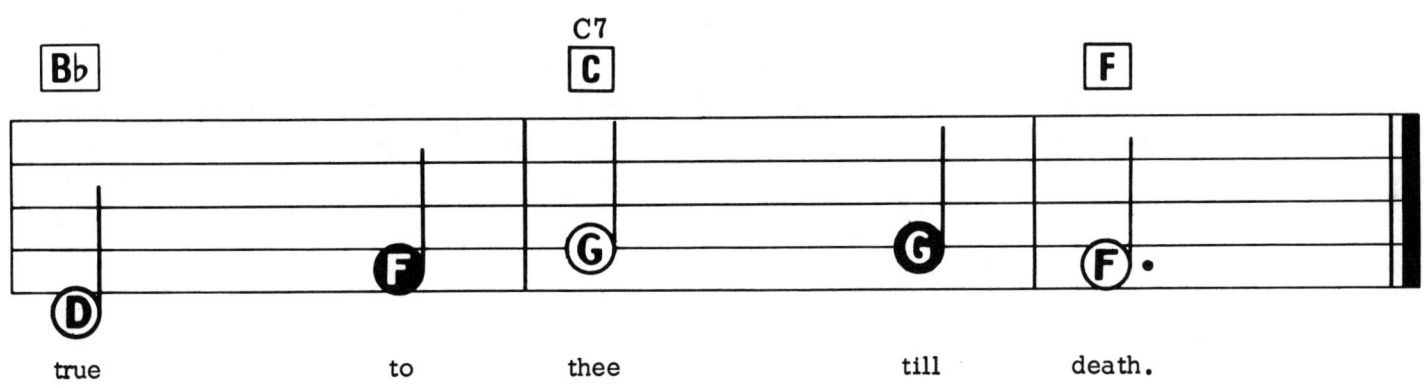

Give Me That Old Time Religion

Registration 5
Rhythm: Swing

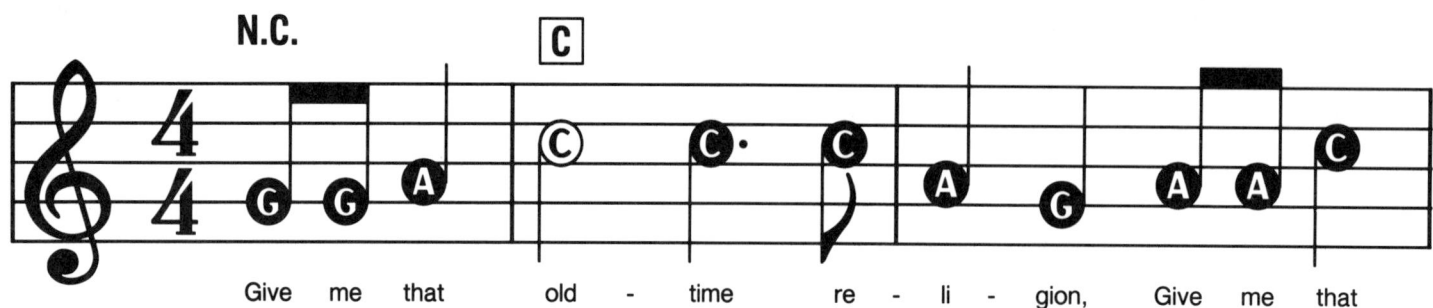

Give me that old-time re-li-gion, Give me that

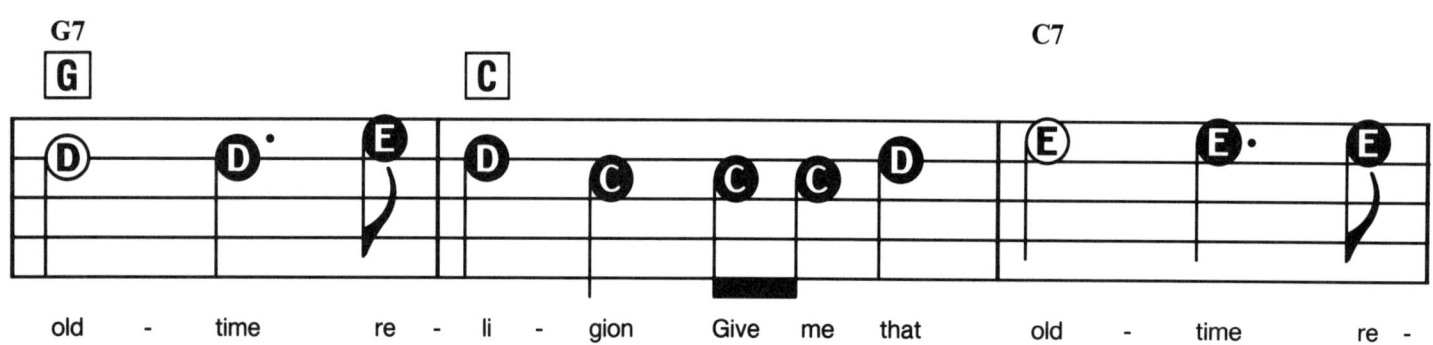

old-time re-li-gion Give me that old-time re-

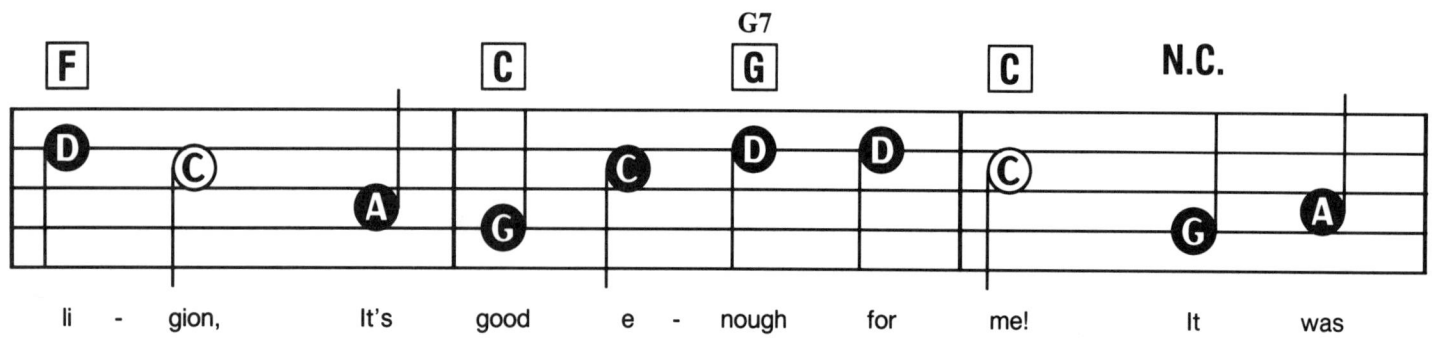

li-gion, It's good e-nough for me! It was

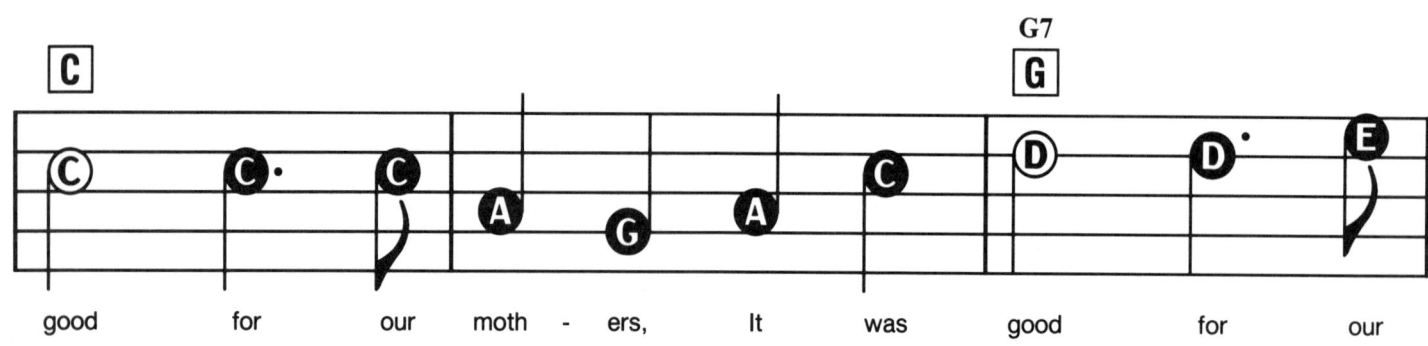

good for our moth-ers, It was good for our

Copyright © 1991 by HAL LEONARD PUBLISHING CORPORATION
International Copyright Secured   All Rights Reserved

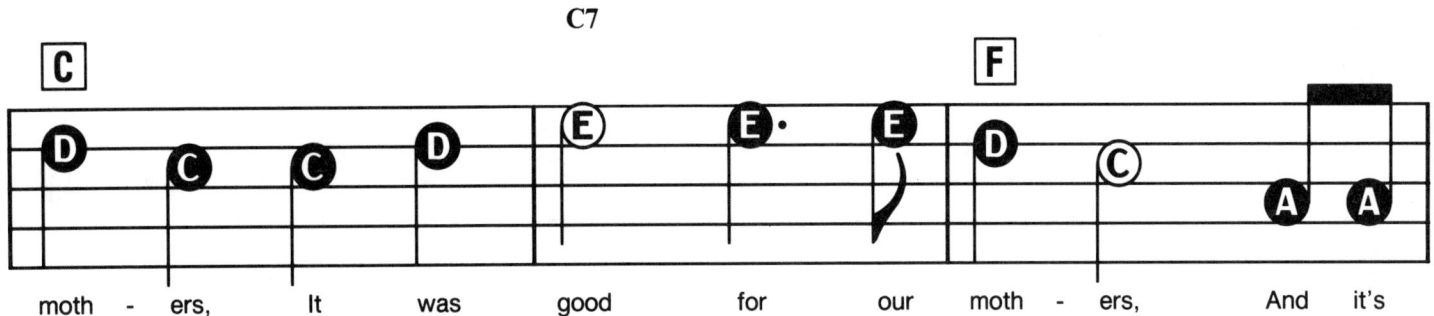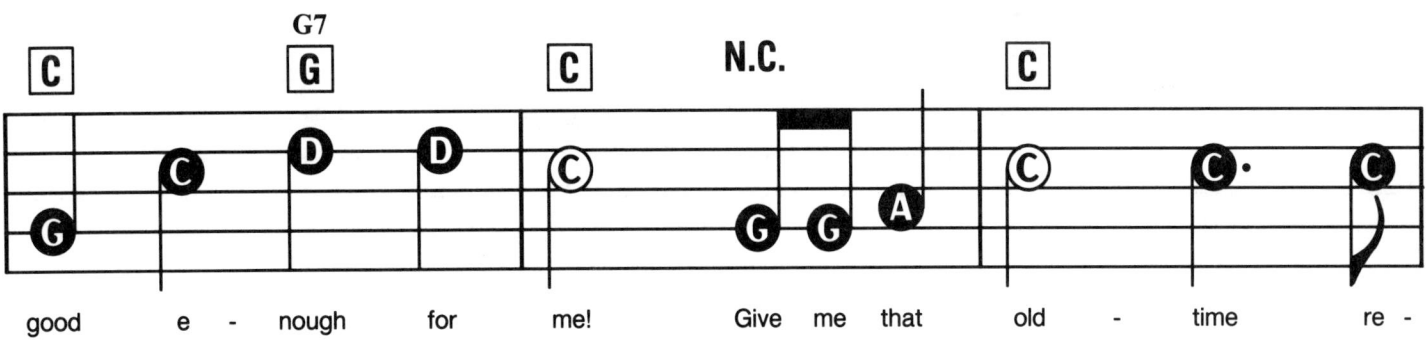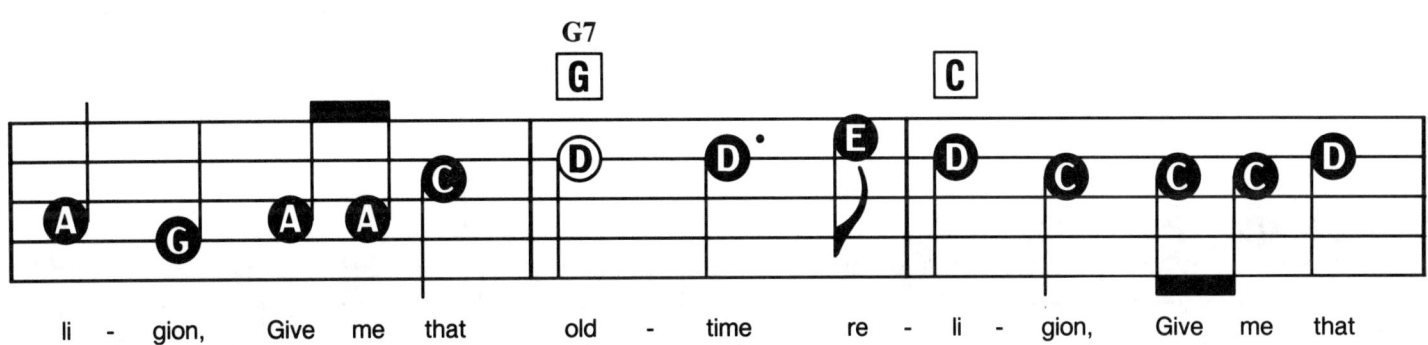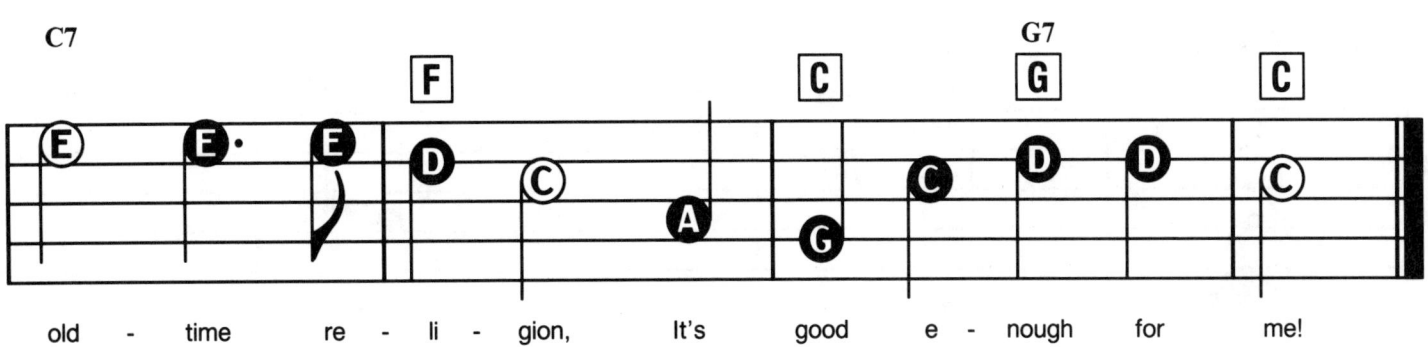

In The Garden

Registration 2
Rhythm: Waltz

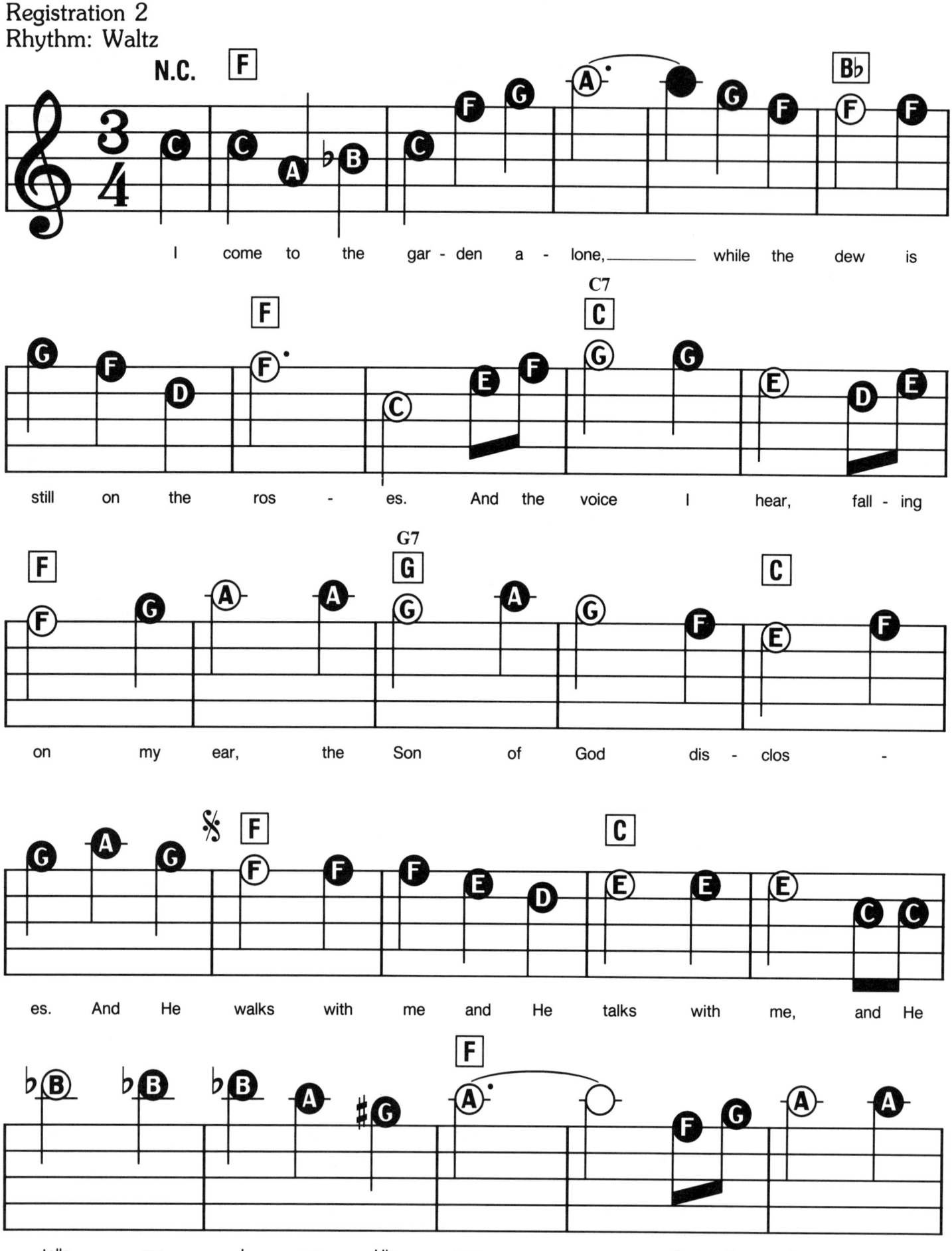

Copyright © 1991 by HAL LEONARD PUBLISHING CORPORATION
International Copyright Secured   All Rights Reserved

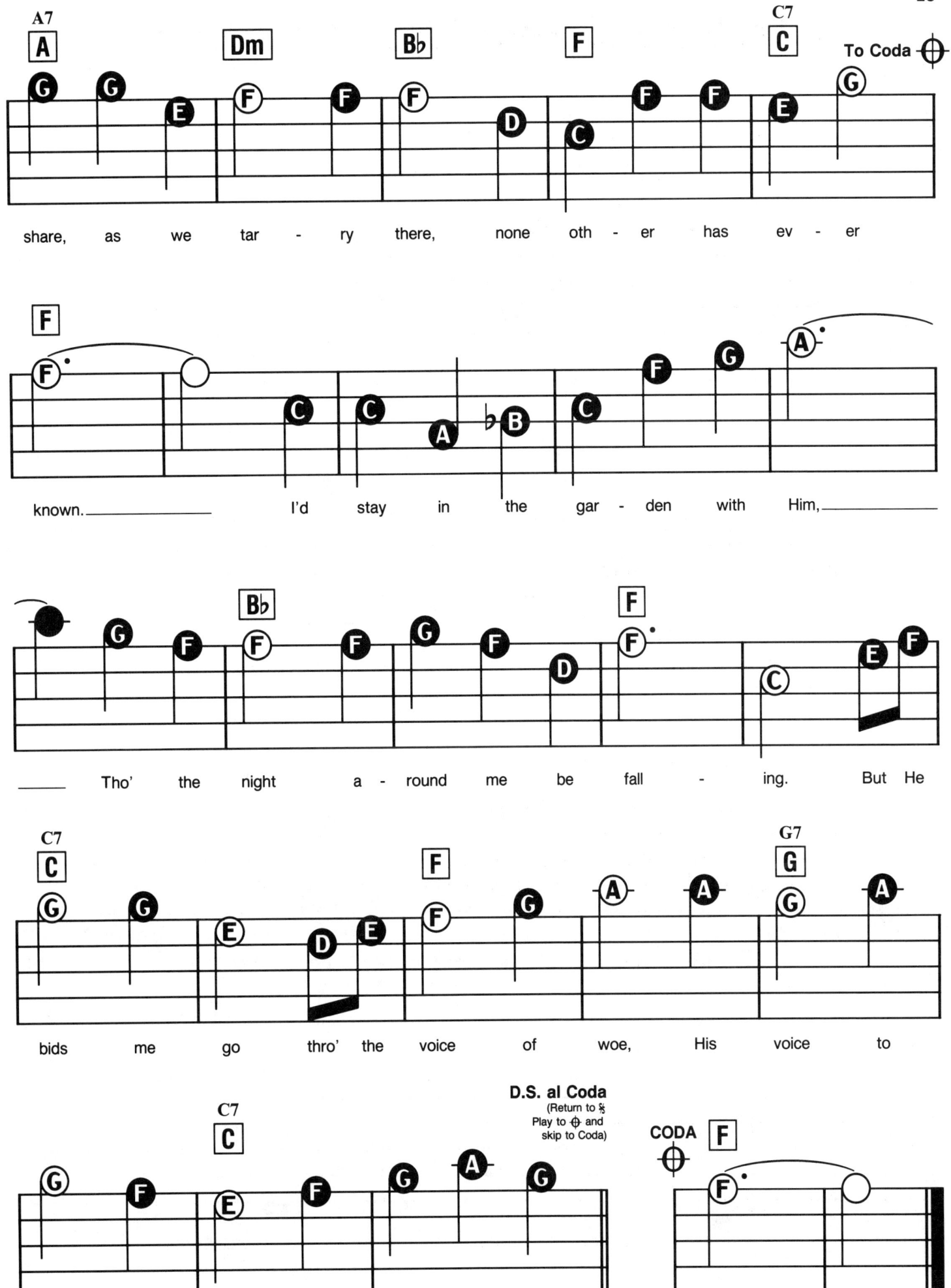

In The Sweet Bye And Bye

Registration 1

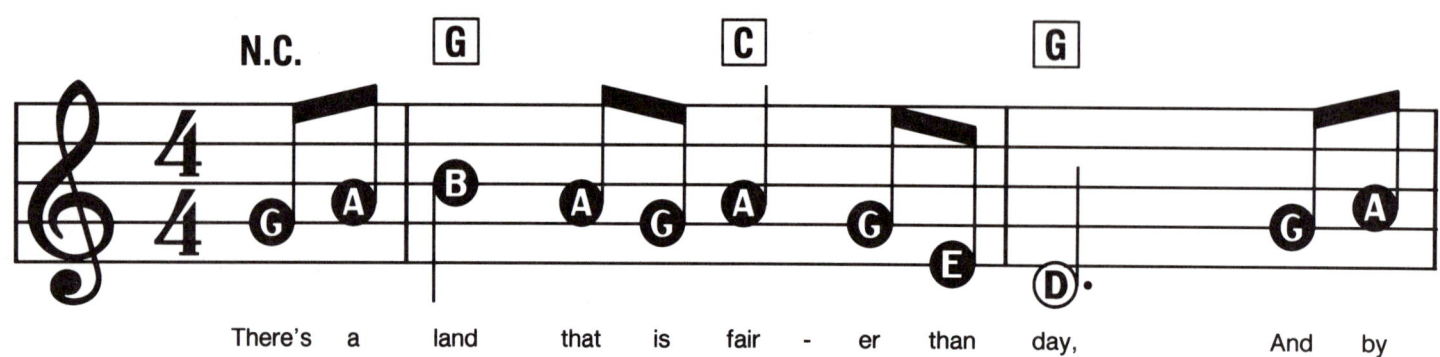
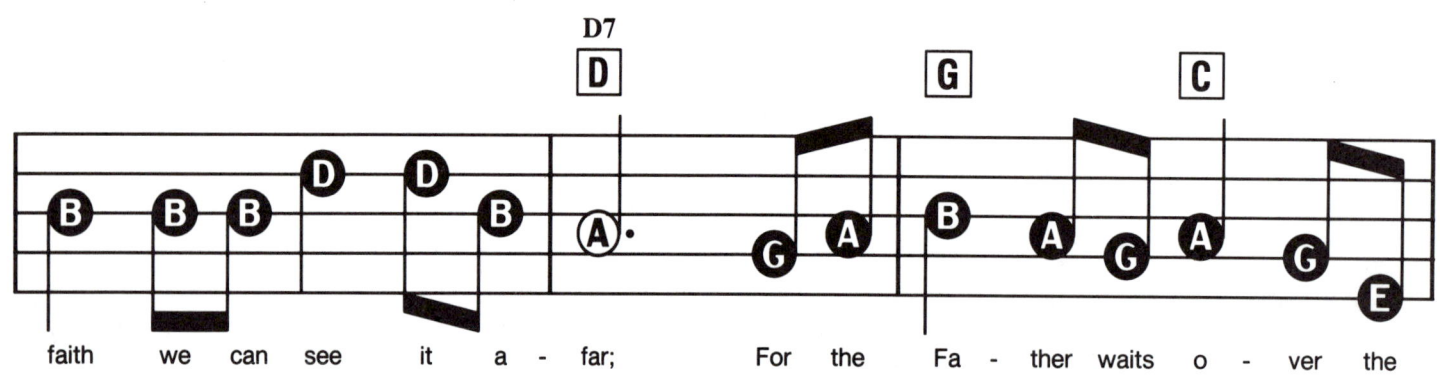
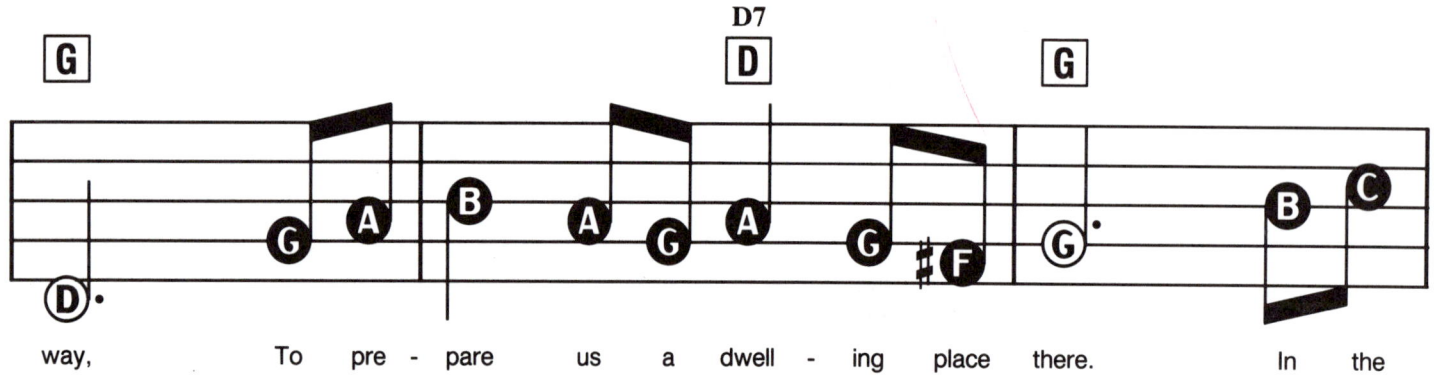
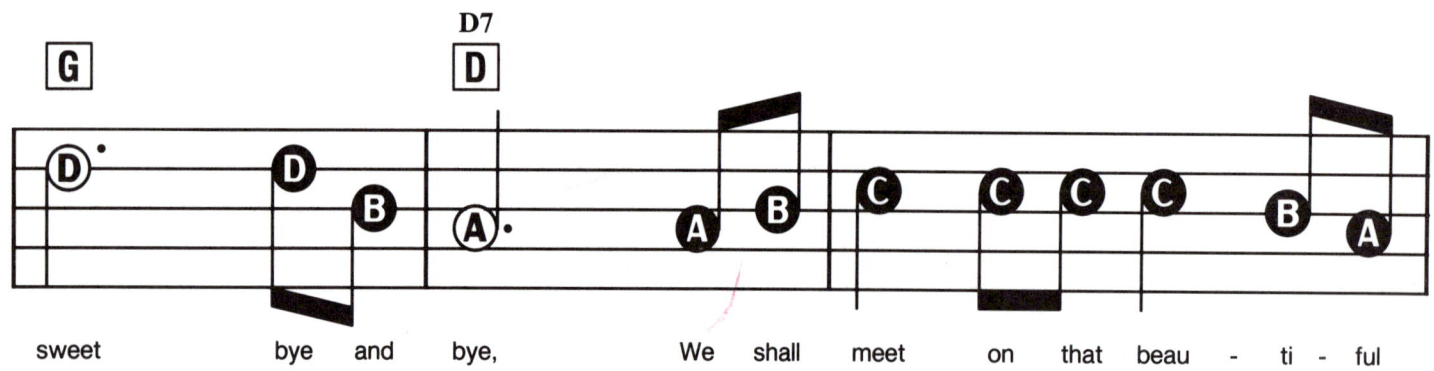

Copyright © 1991 by HAL LEONARD PUBLISHING CORPORATION
International Copyright Secured   All Rights Reserved

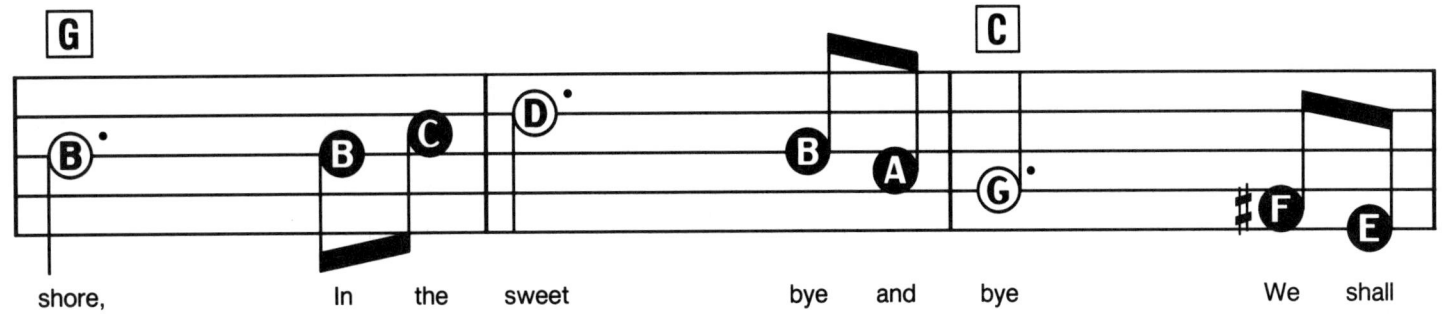
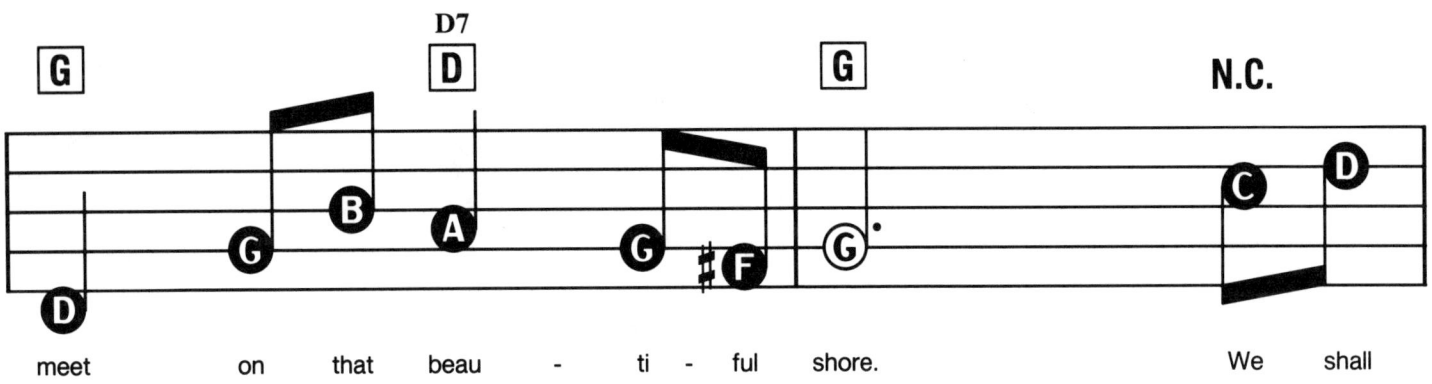
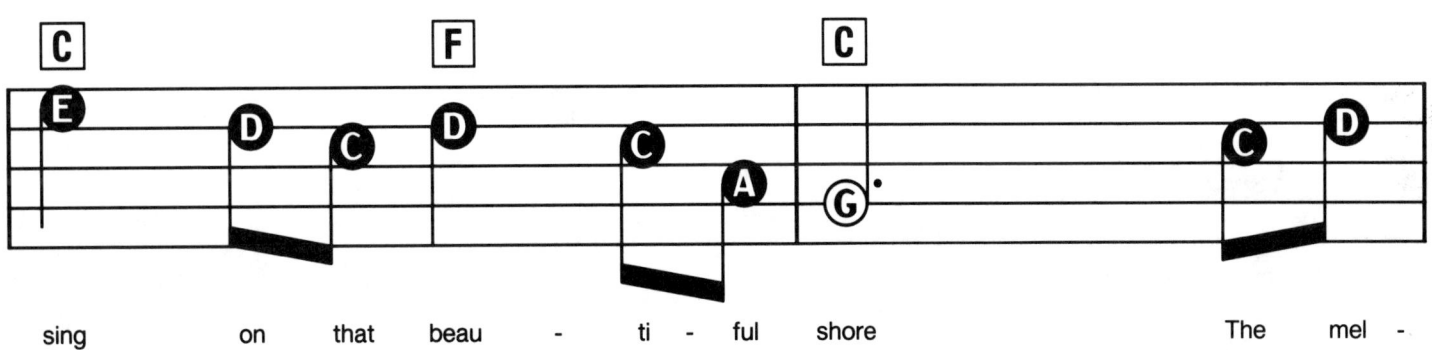
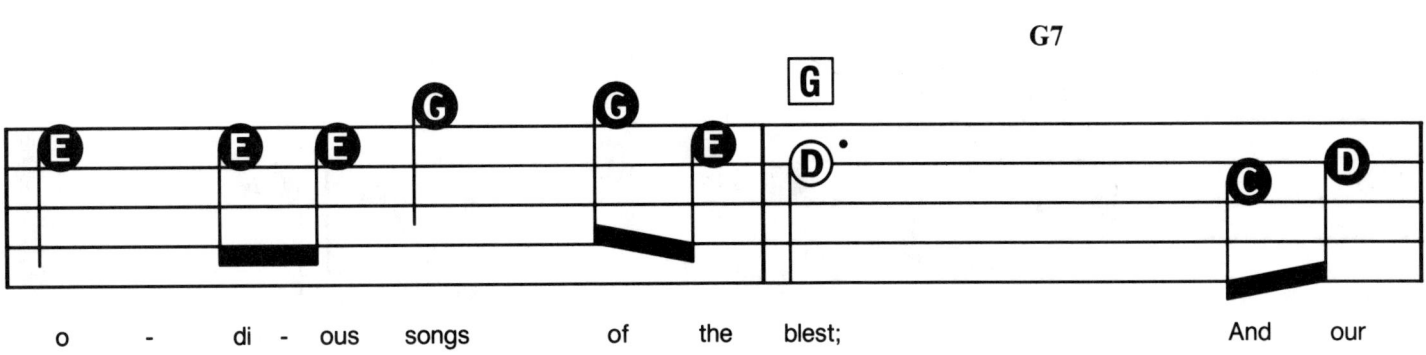

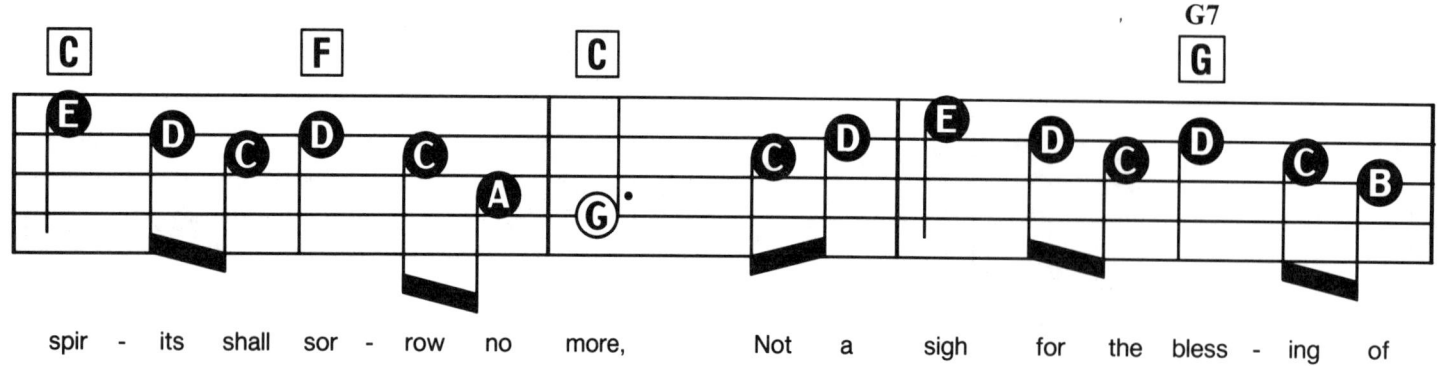
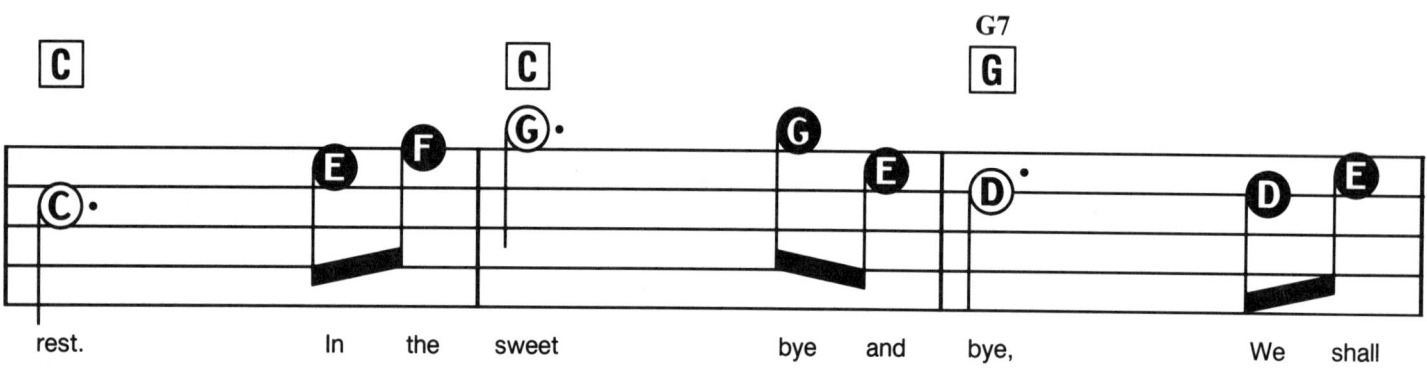
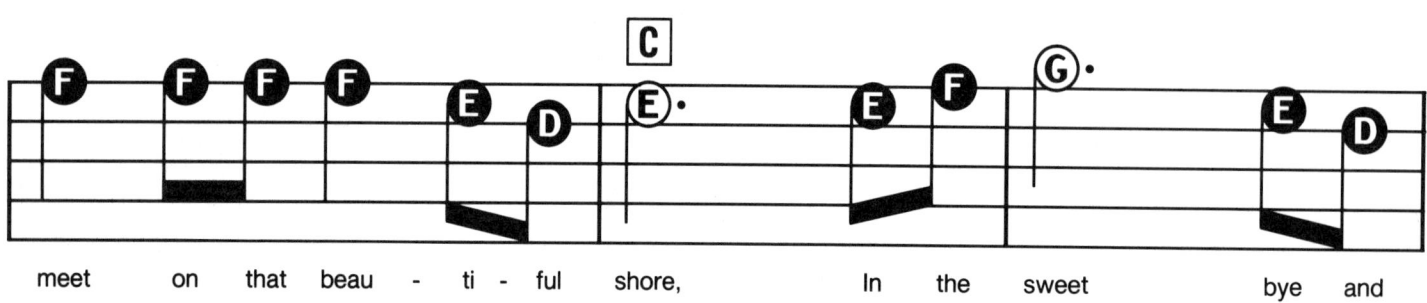
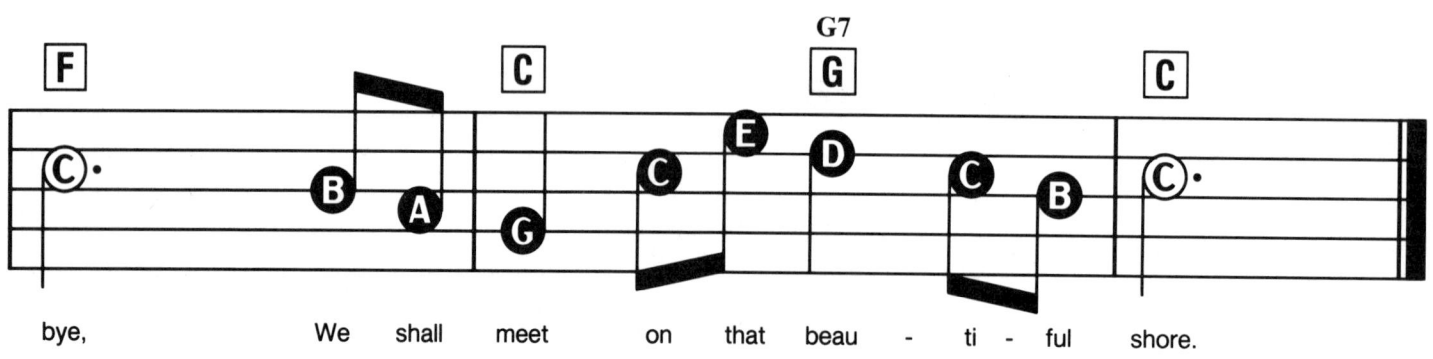

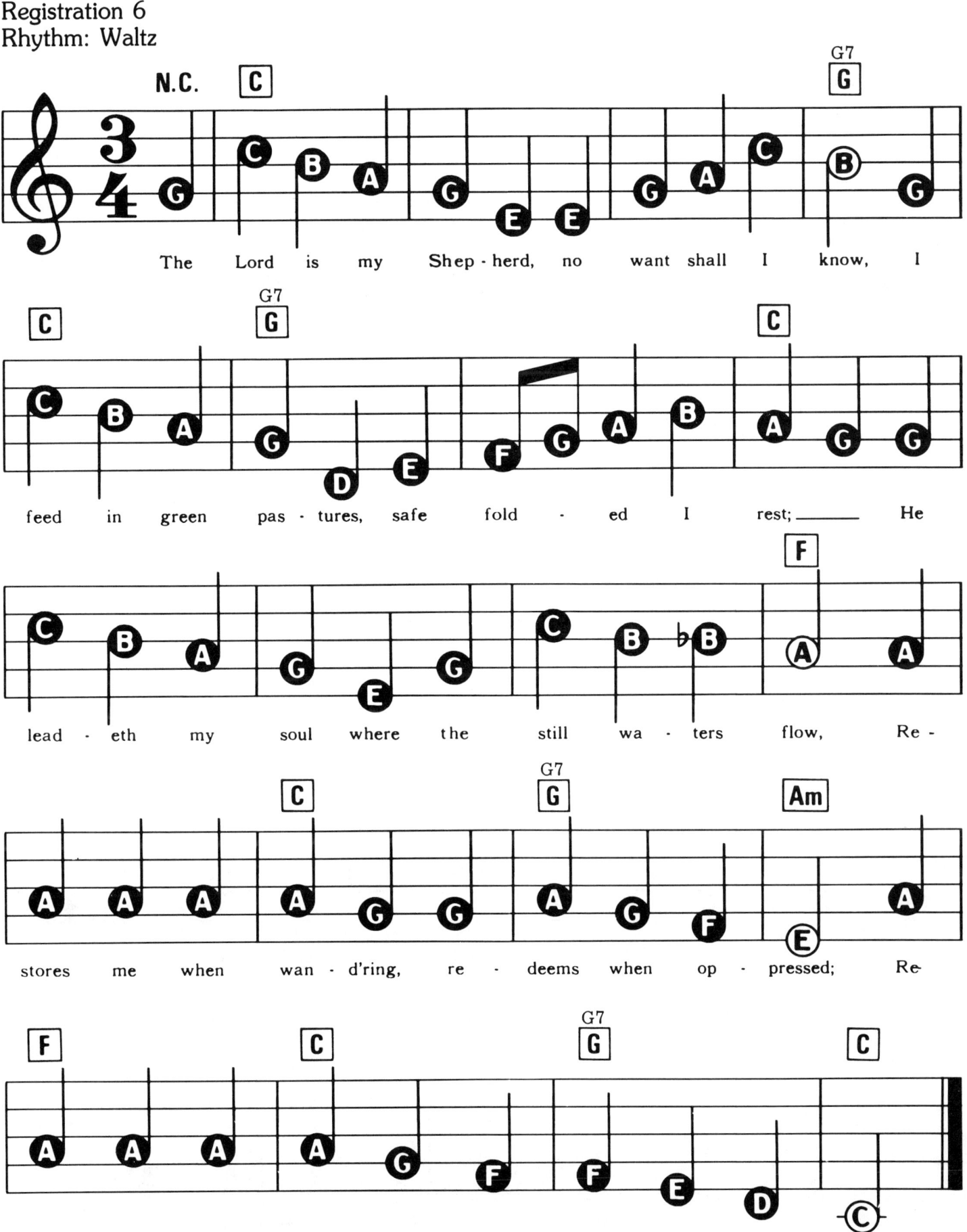

Jesus, Lover Of My Soul

Registration 3
Rhythm: Waltz

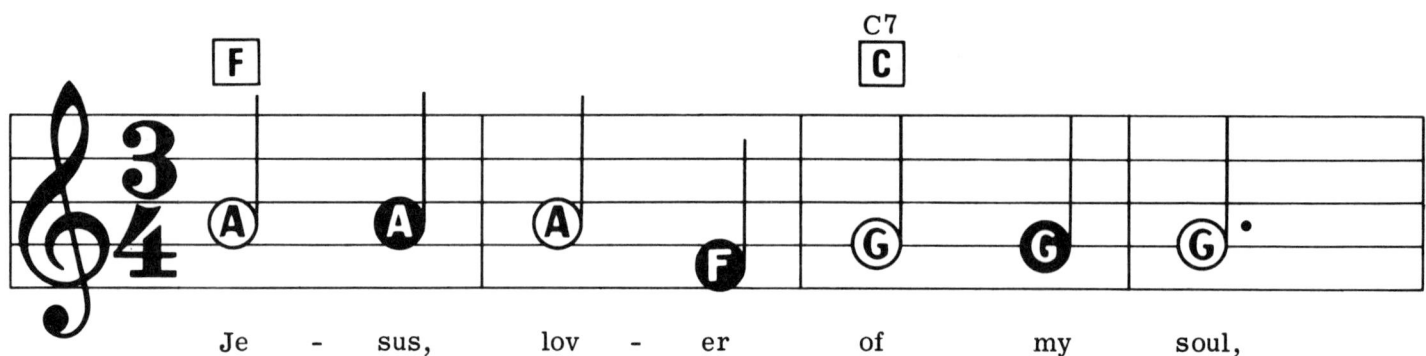

Je - sus, lov - er of my soul,

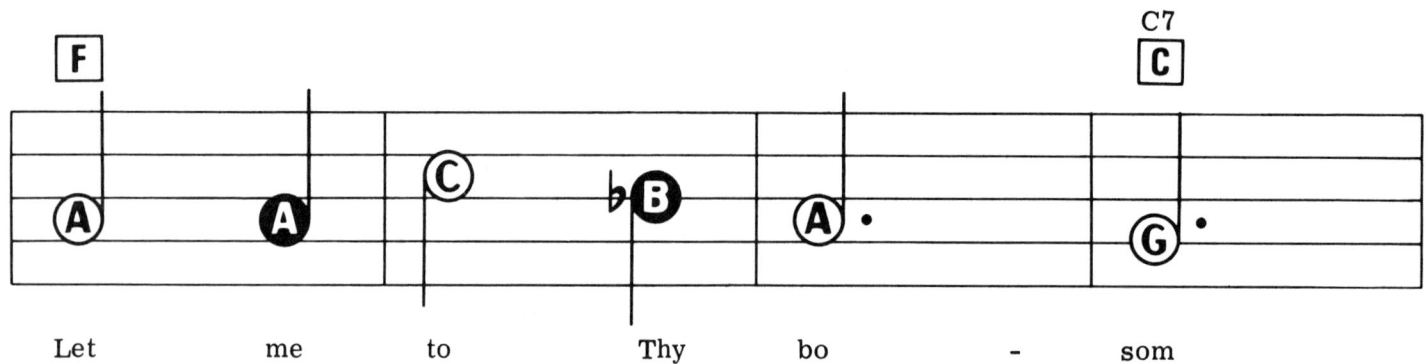

Let me to Thy bo - som

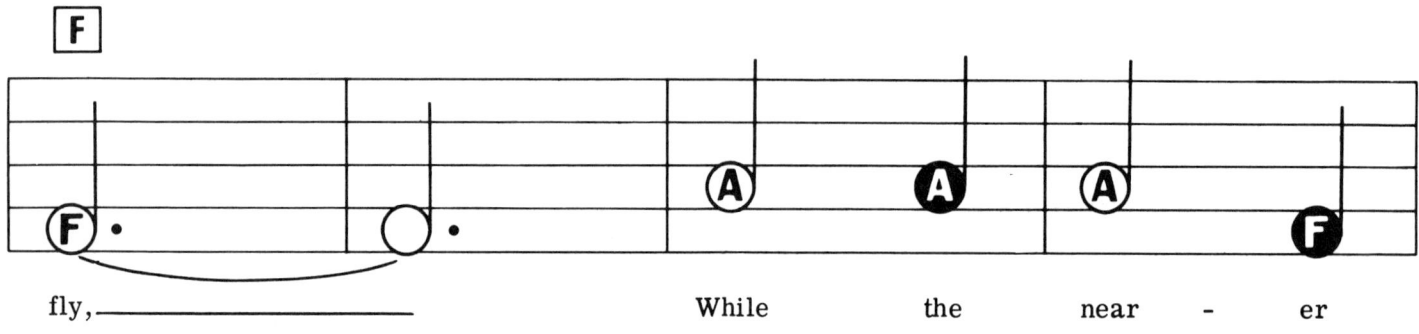

fly,_____ While the near - er

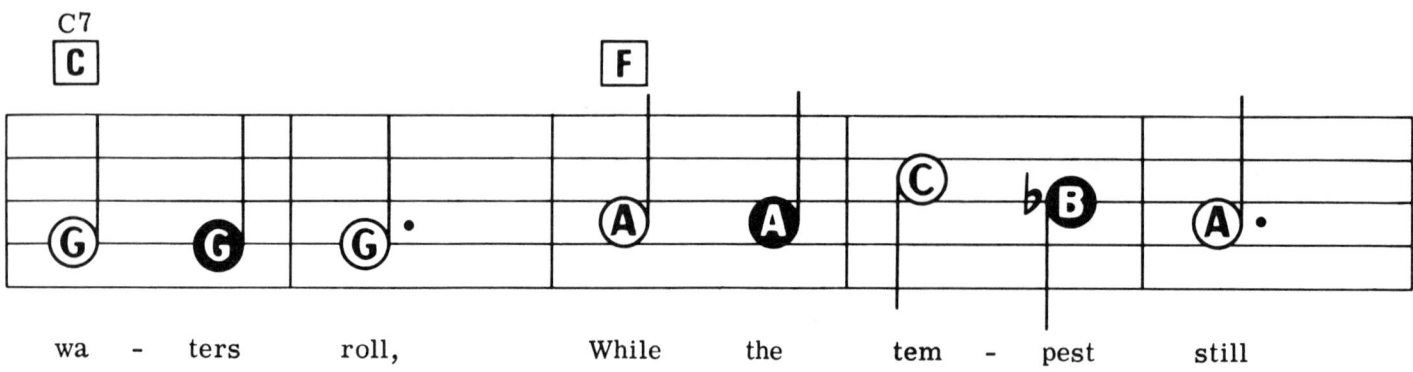

wa - ters roll, While the tem - pest still

This arr. © Copyright 1975 by HAL LEONARD PUBLISHING CORPORATION, Winona, MN 55987
Made in U.S.A.   International Copyright Secured   All Rights Reserved

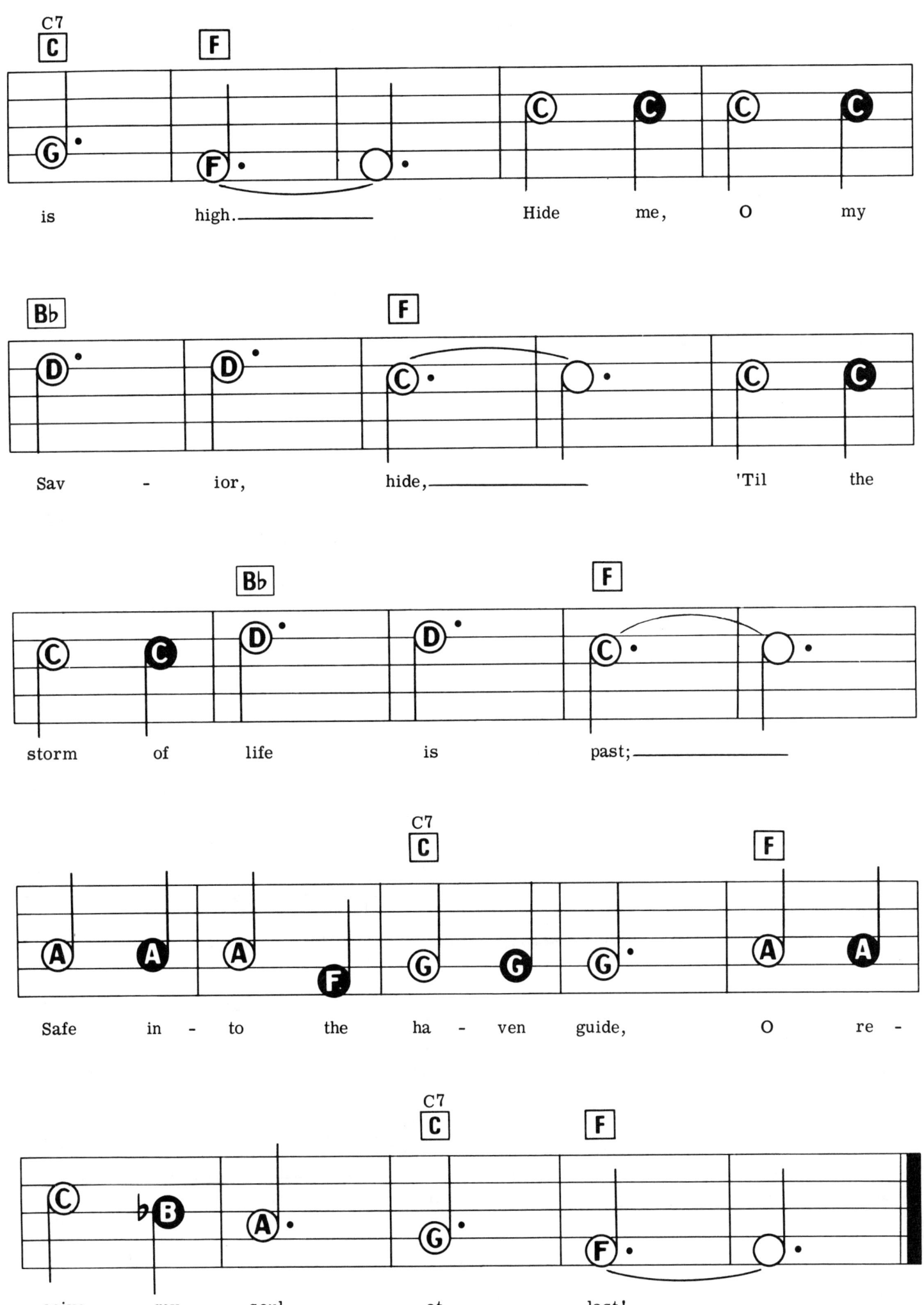

Joshua Fit The Battle Of Jericho

Registration 6
Rhythm: Swing

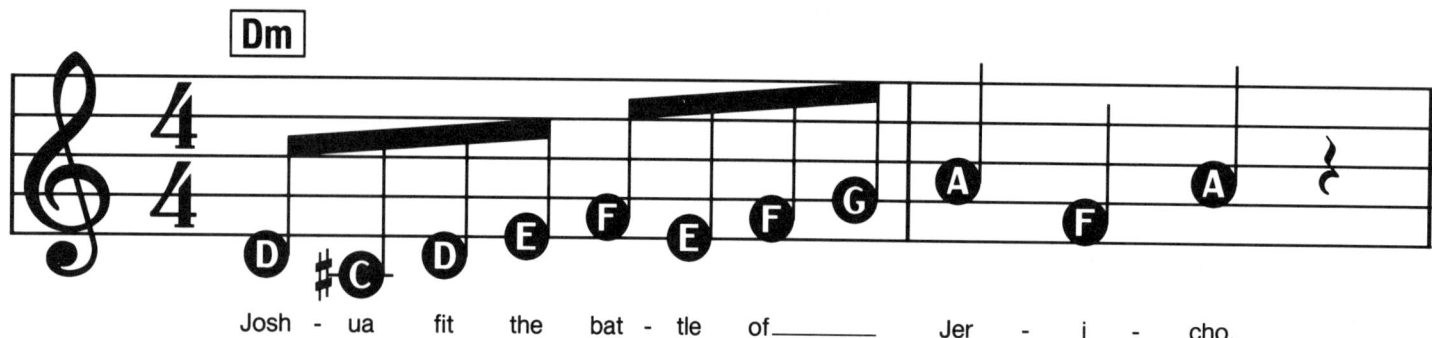
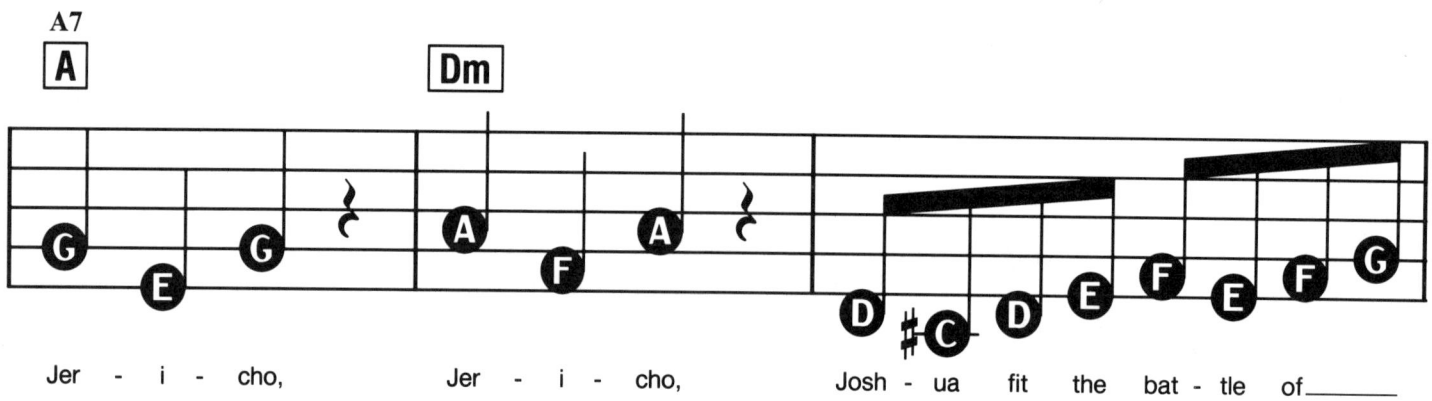
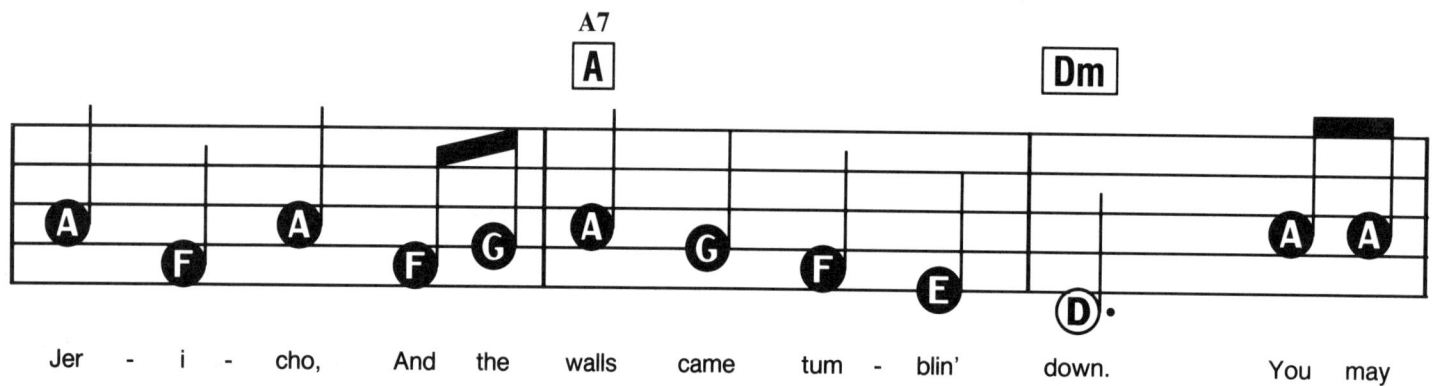
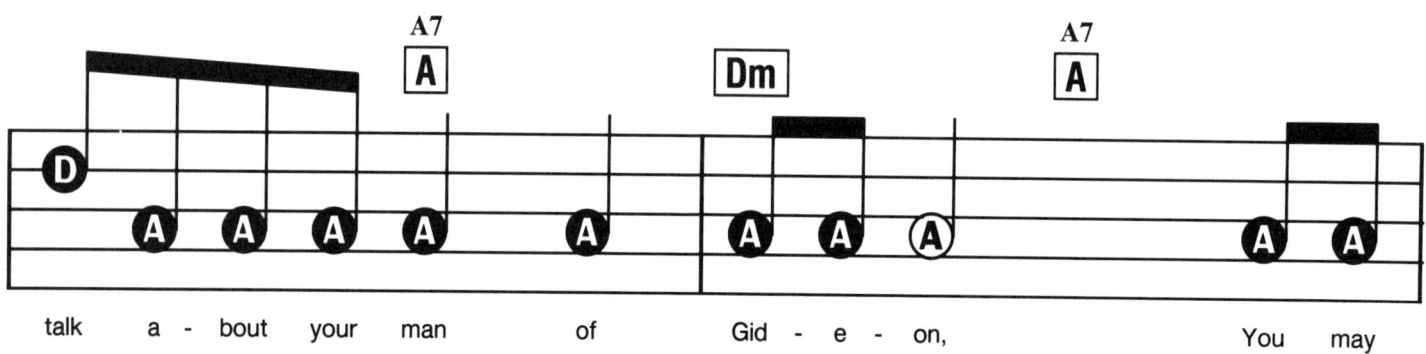

Copyright © 1991 by HAL LEONARD PUBLISHING CORPORATION
International Copyright Secured   All Rights Reserved

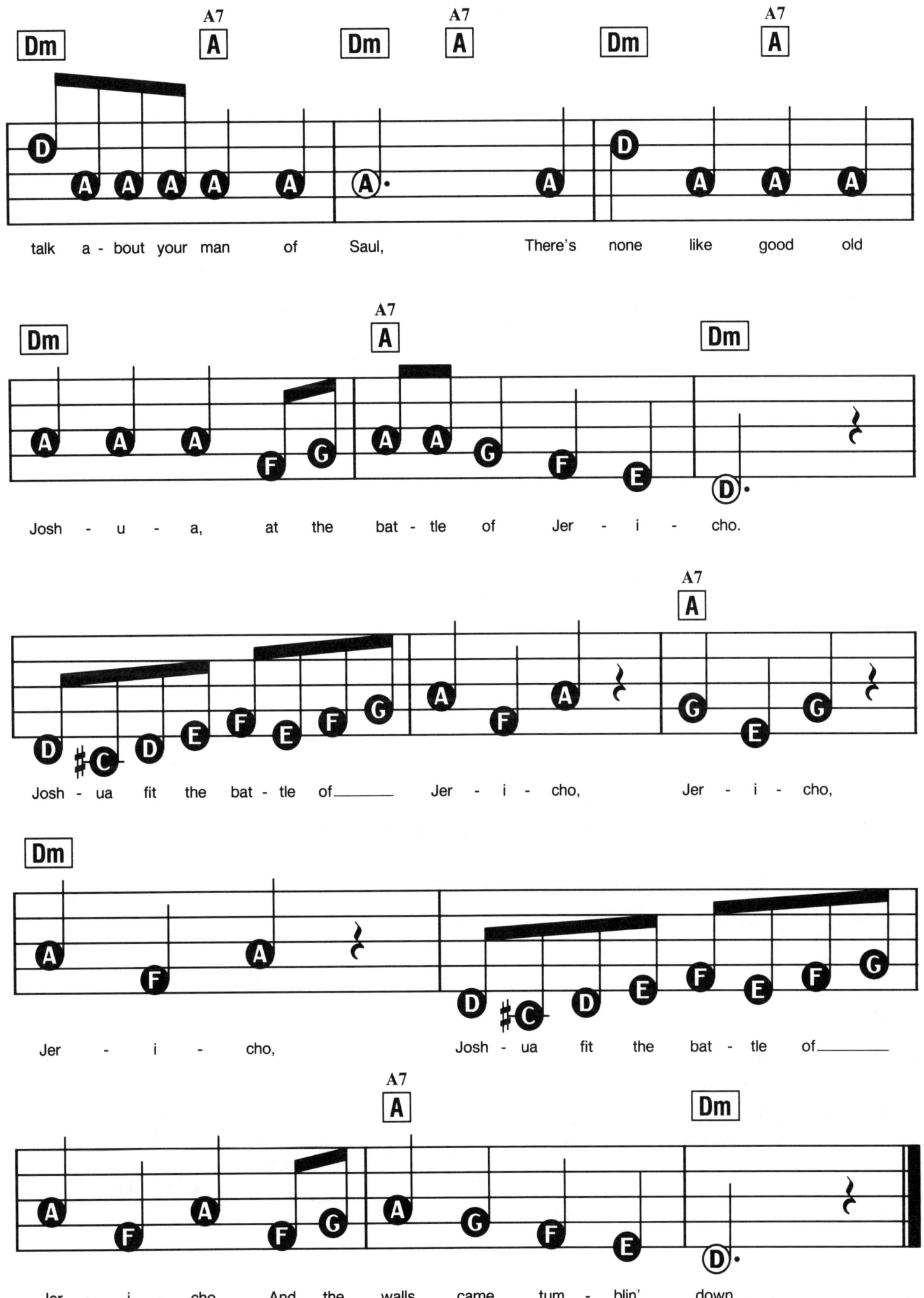

Nearer, My God, To Thee

Registration 2

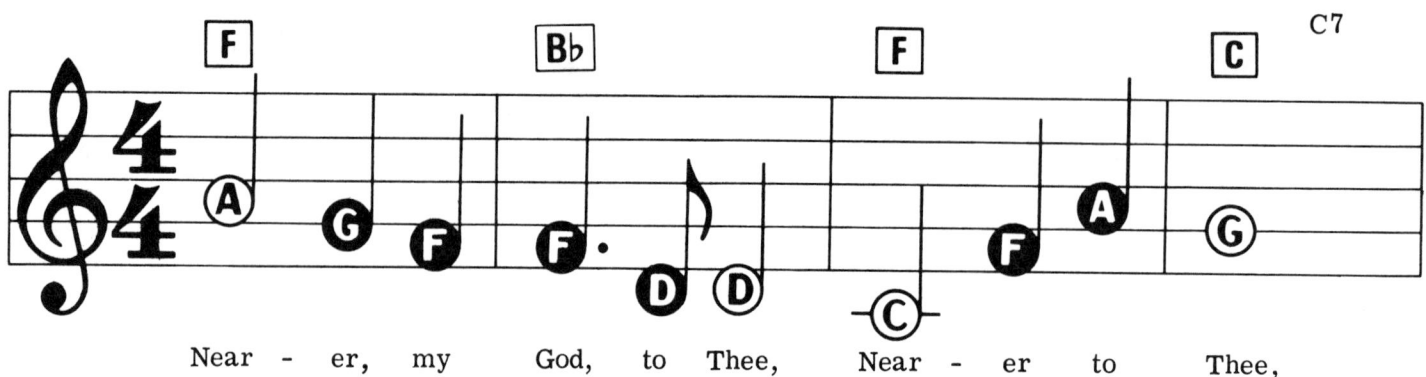

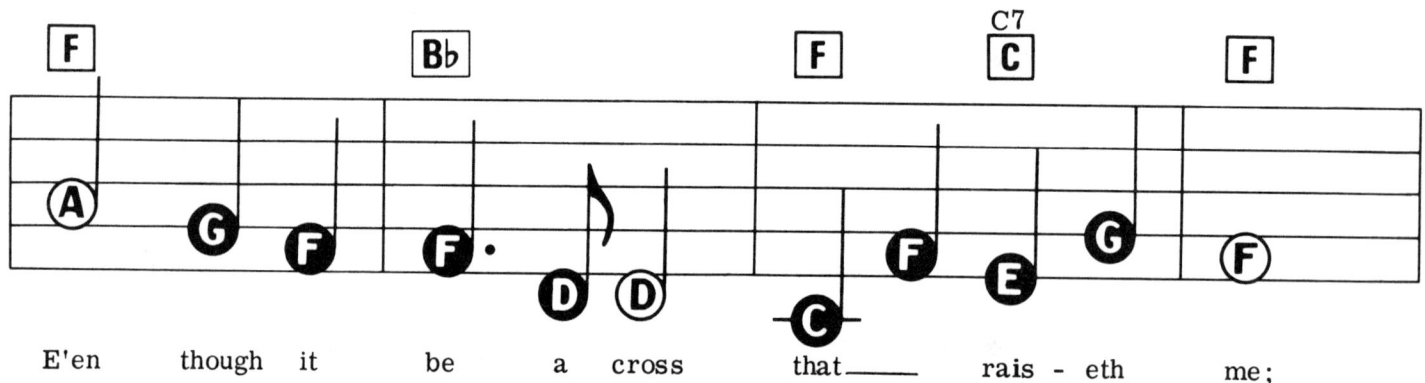

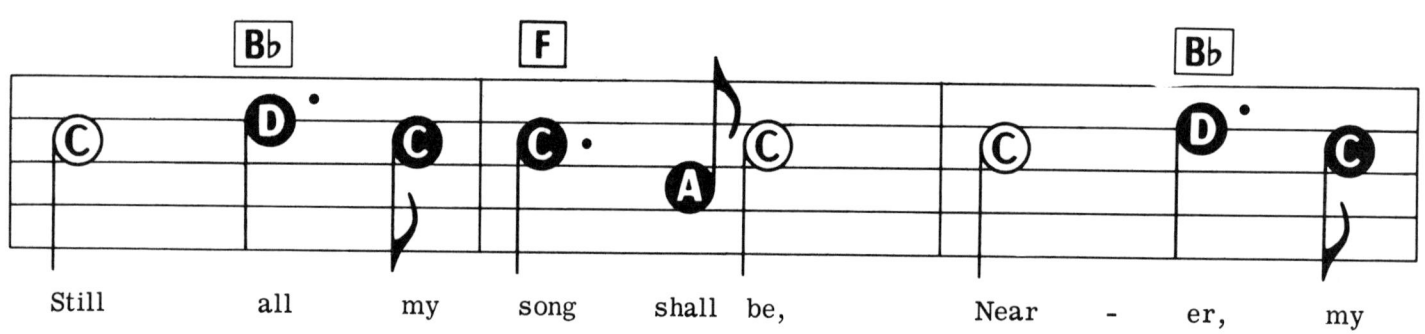

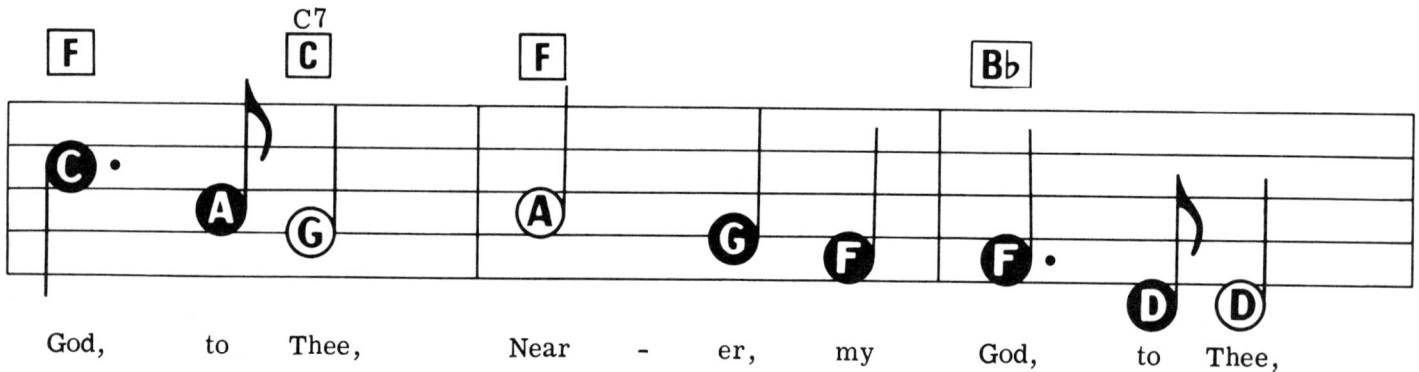

This arr. © Copyright 1975 by HAL LEONARD PUBLISHING CORPORATION, Winona, MN 55987
Made in U.S.A. International Copyright Secured All Rights Reserved

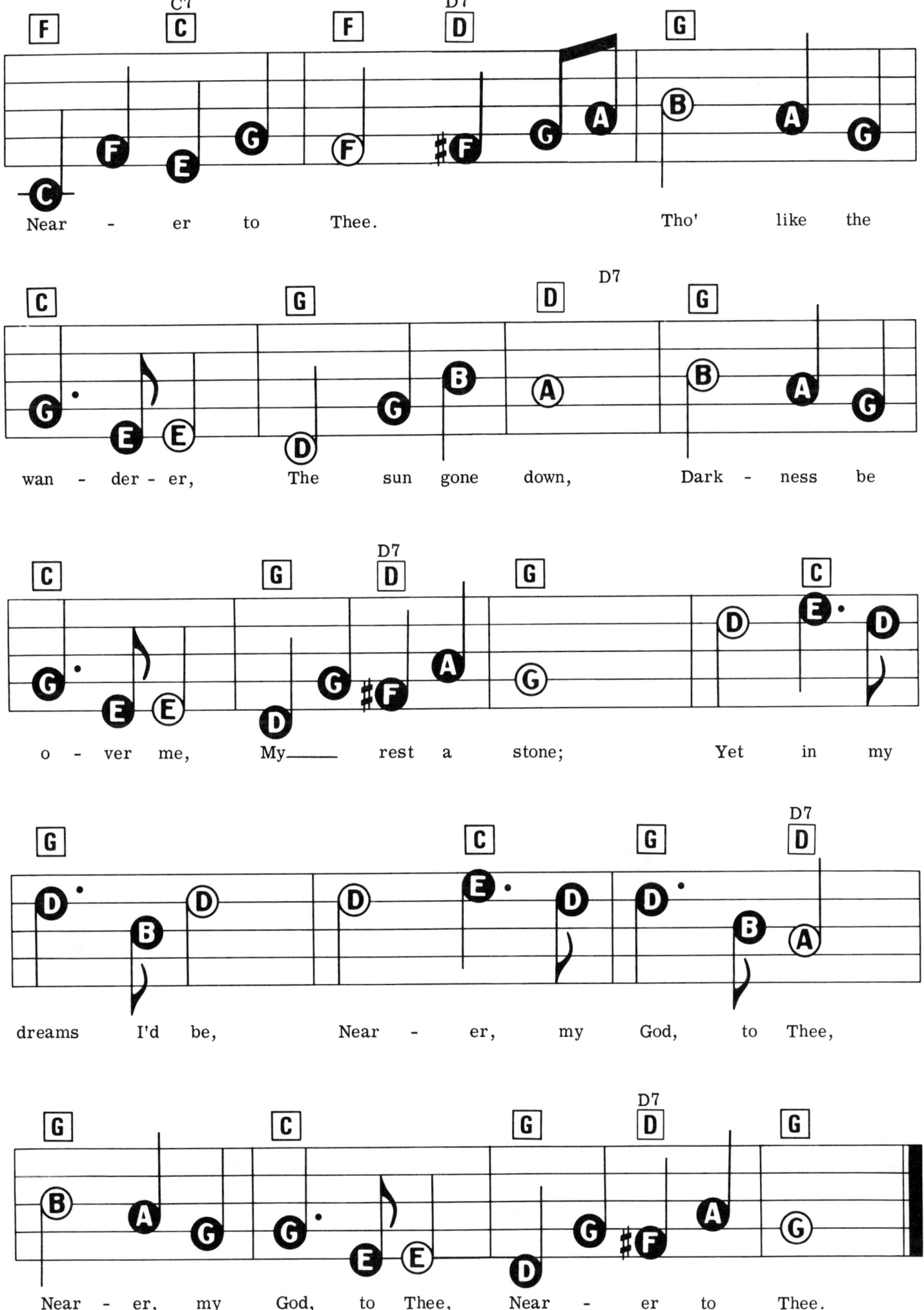

O God, Our Help In Ages Past

Registration 3

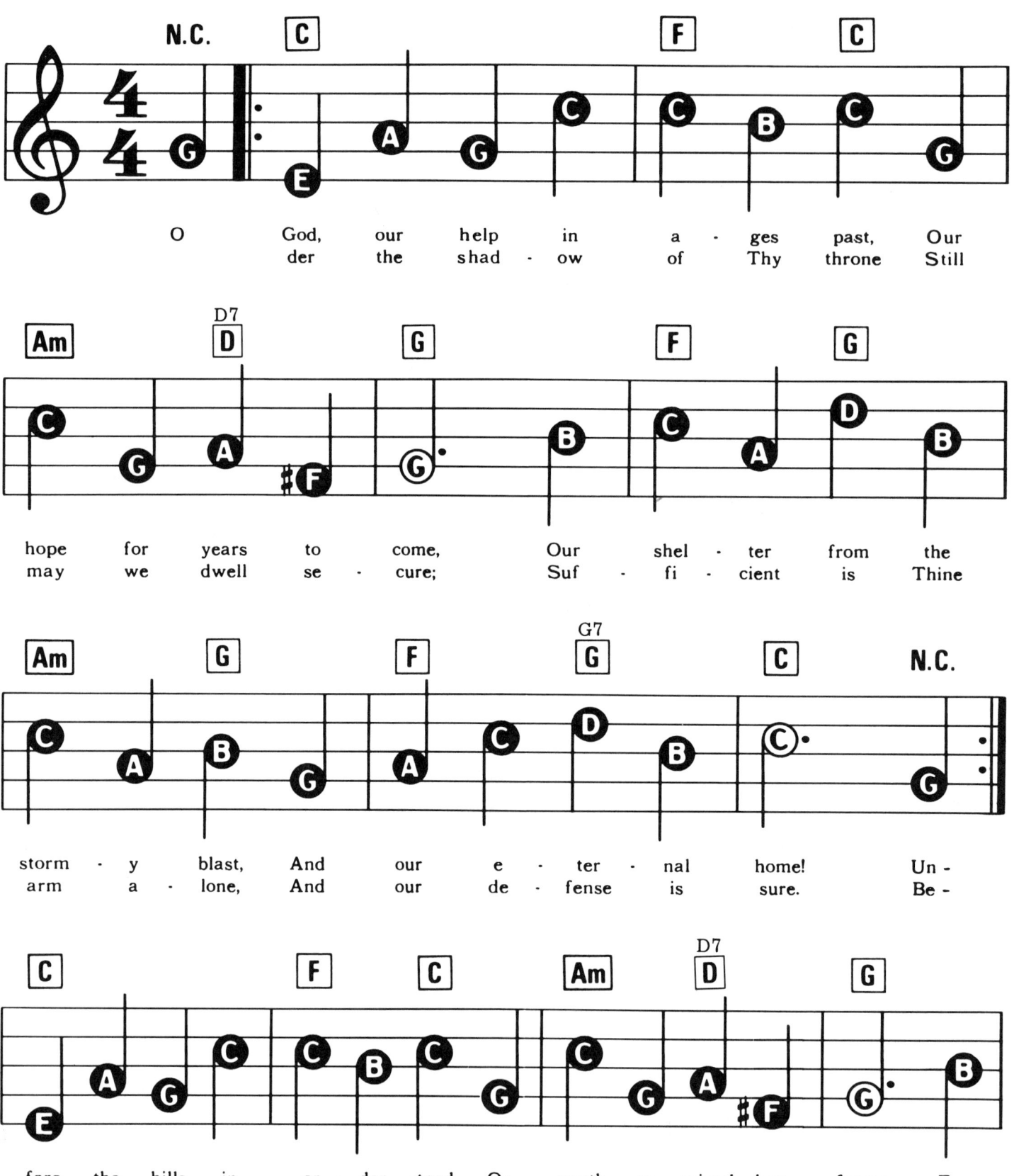

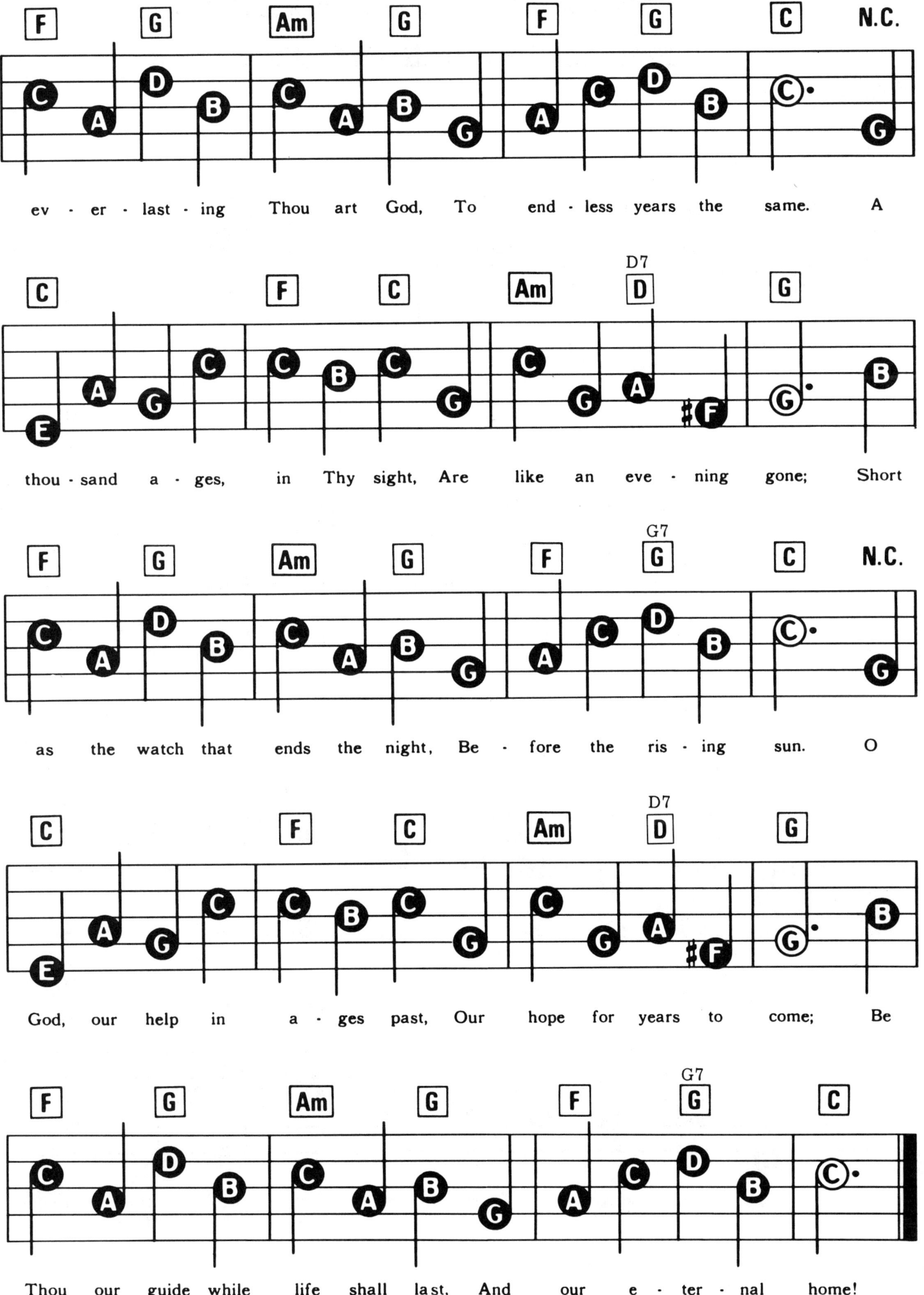

O Worship The King, All Glorious Above

Registration 2

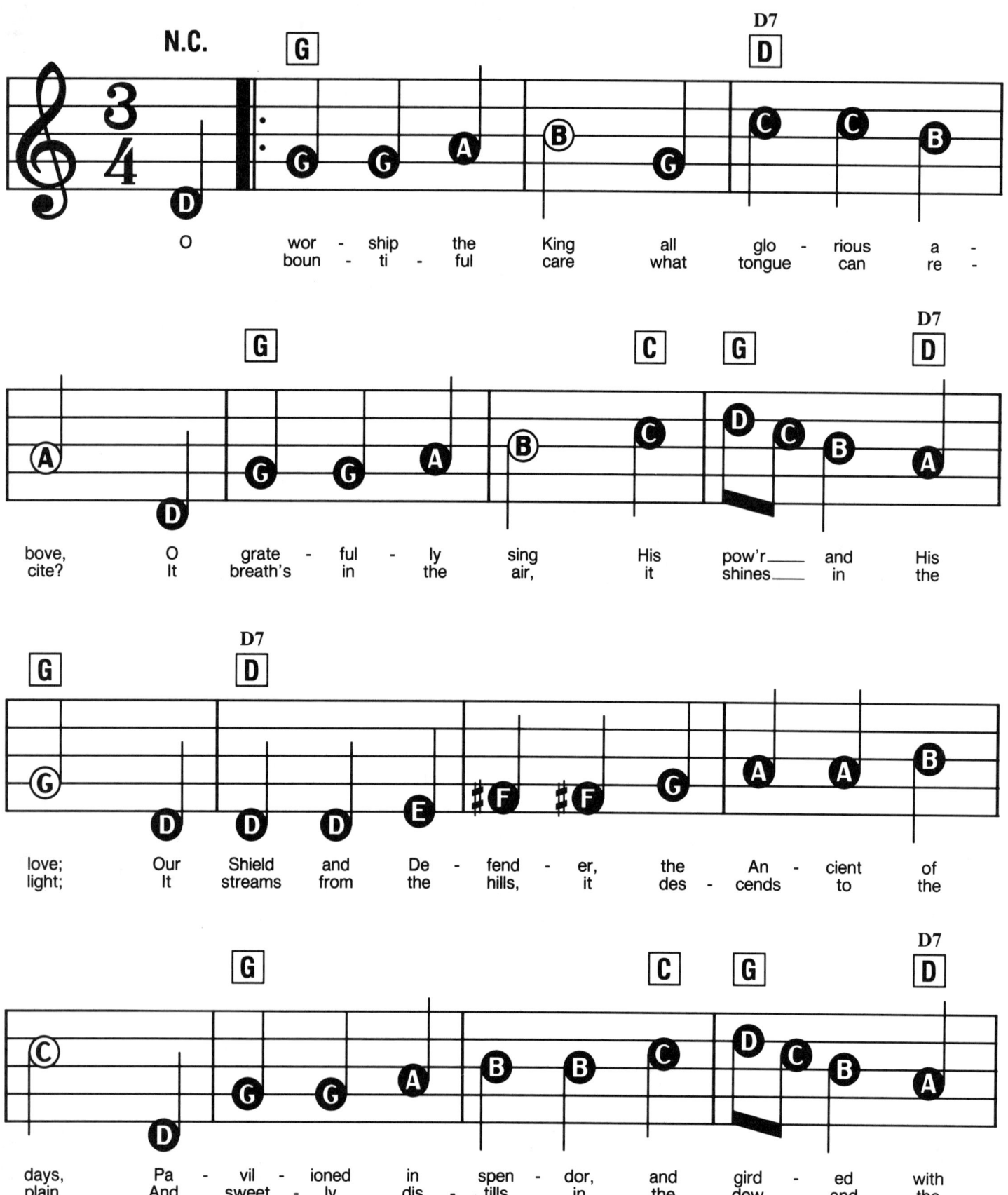

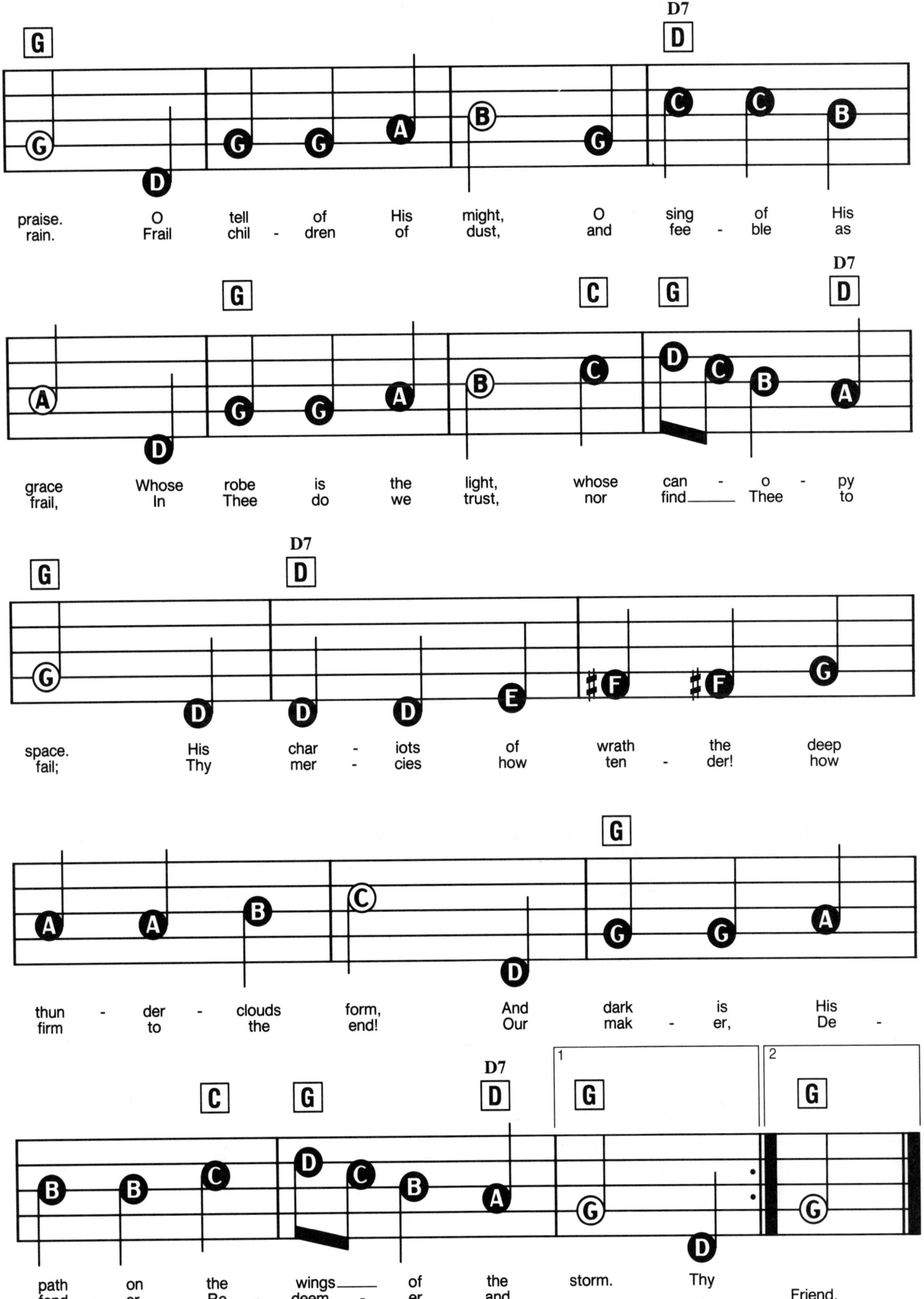

The Old Rugged Cross

Registration 2
Rhythm: Waltz

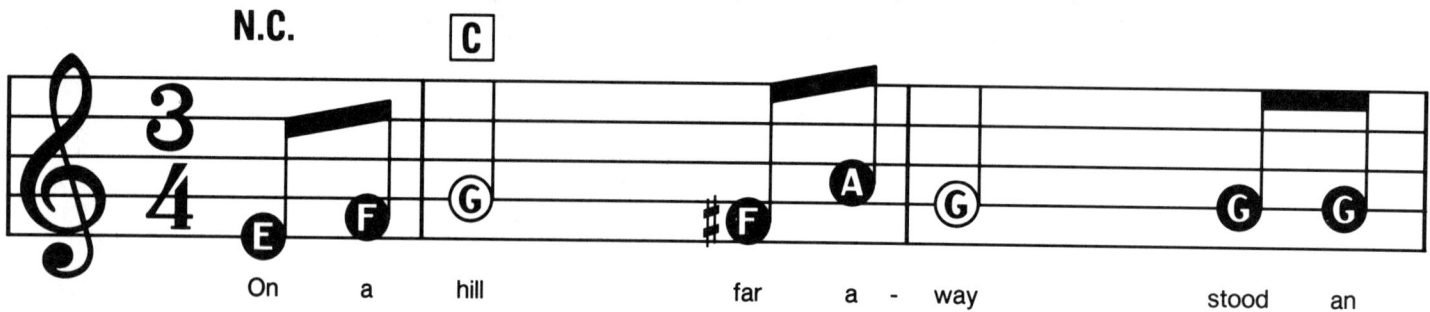
On a hill far a-way stood an

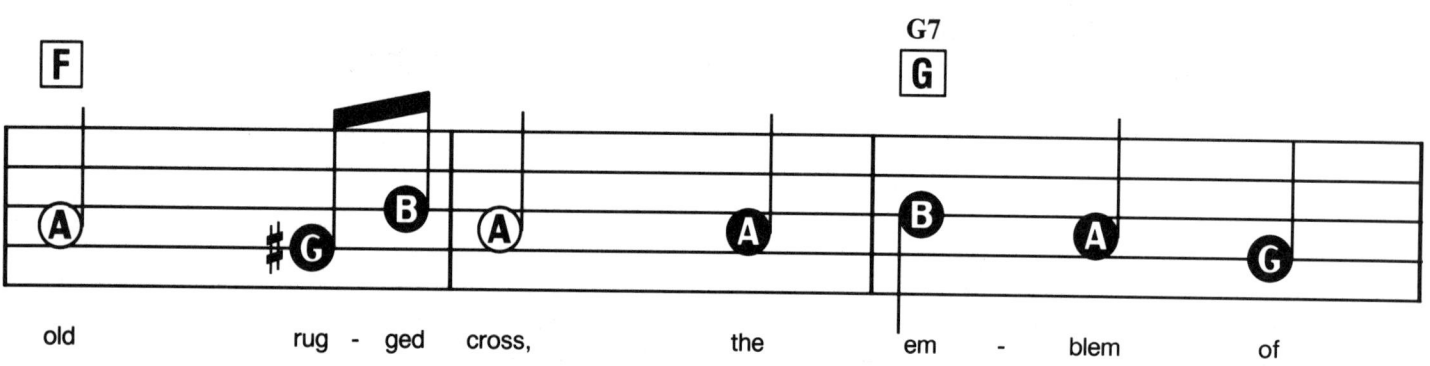
old rug-ged cross, the em-blem of

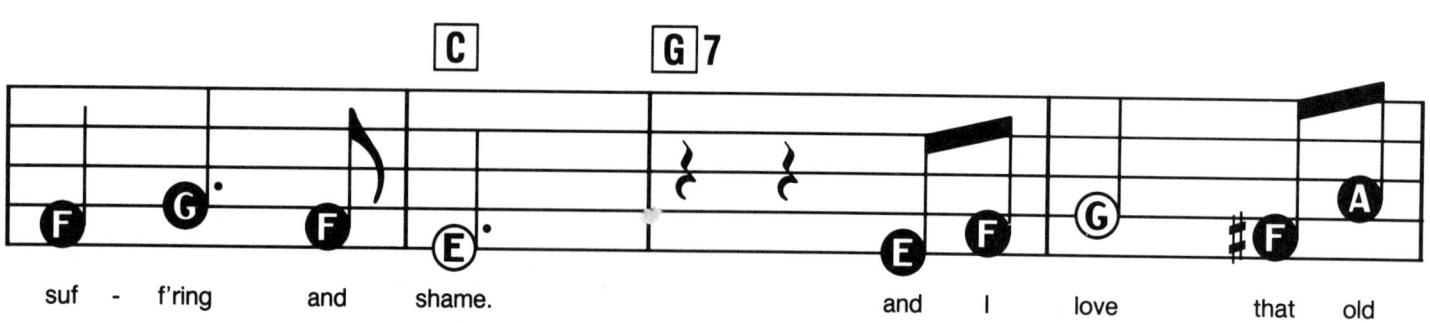
suf-f'ring and shame. and I love that old

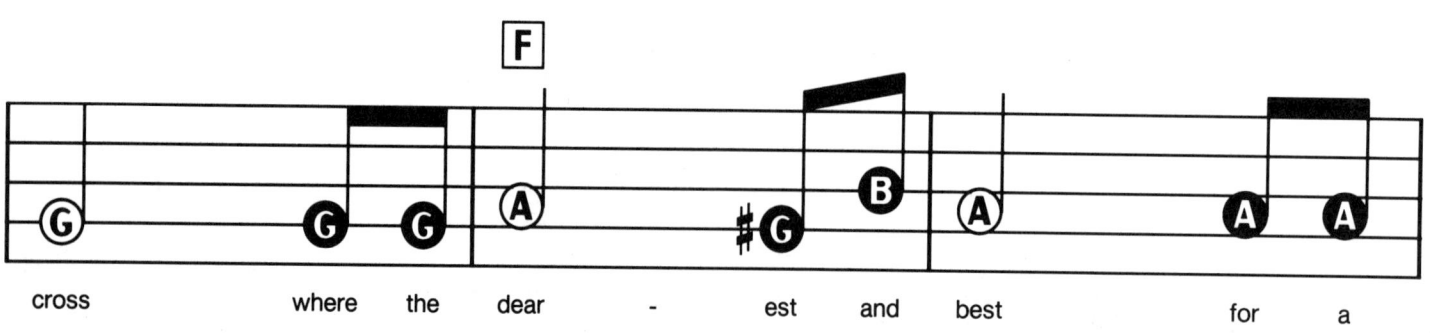
cross where the dear-est and best for a

Copyright © 1991 by HAL LEONARD PUBLISHING CORPORATION
International Copyright Secured   All Rights Reserved

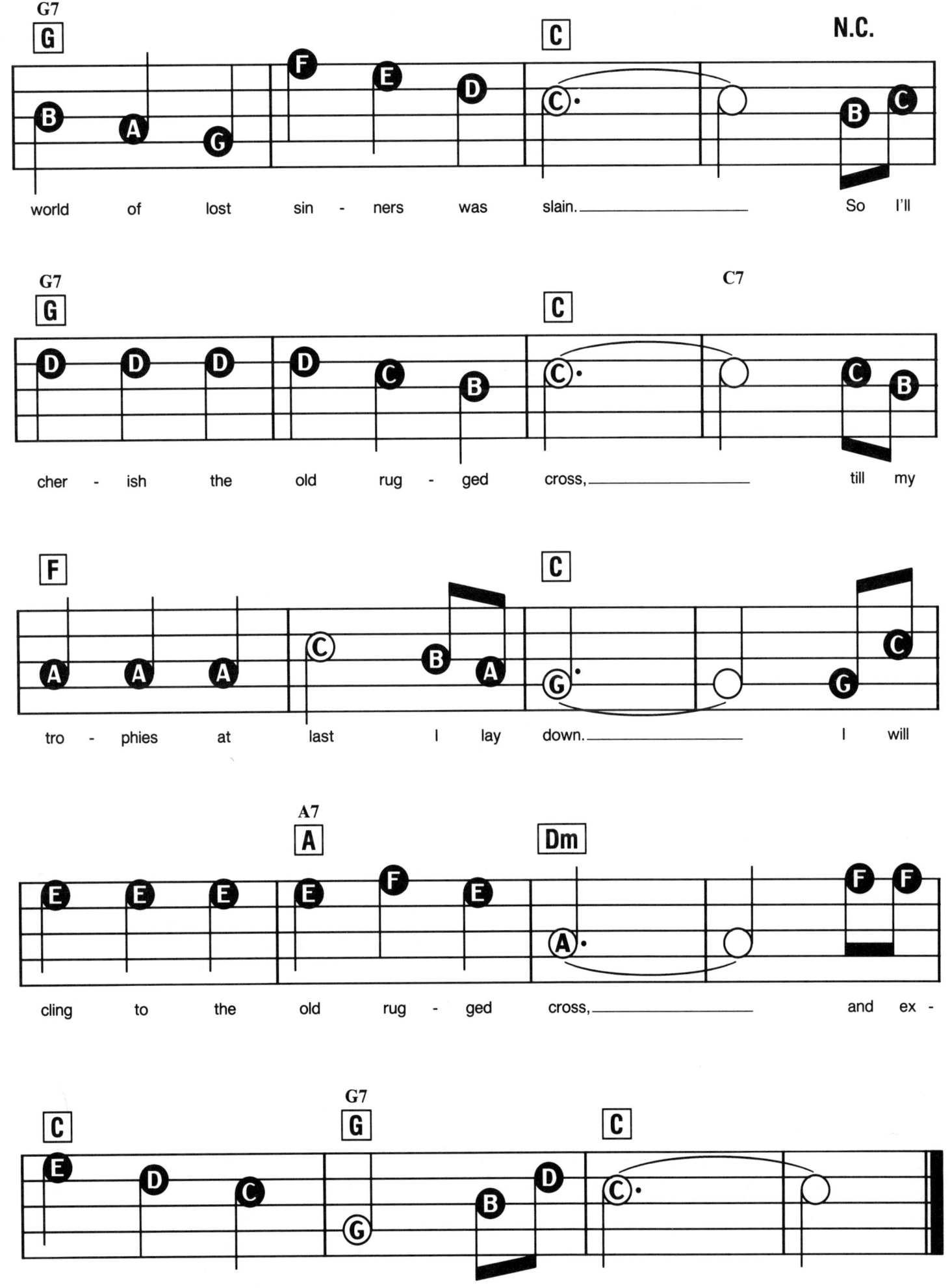

Onward, Christian Soldiers

Registration 6
Rhythm: March

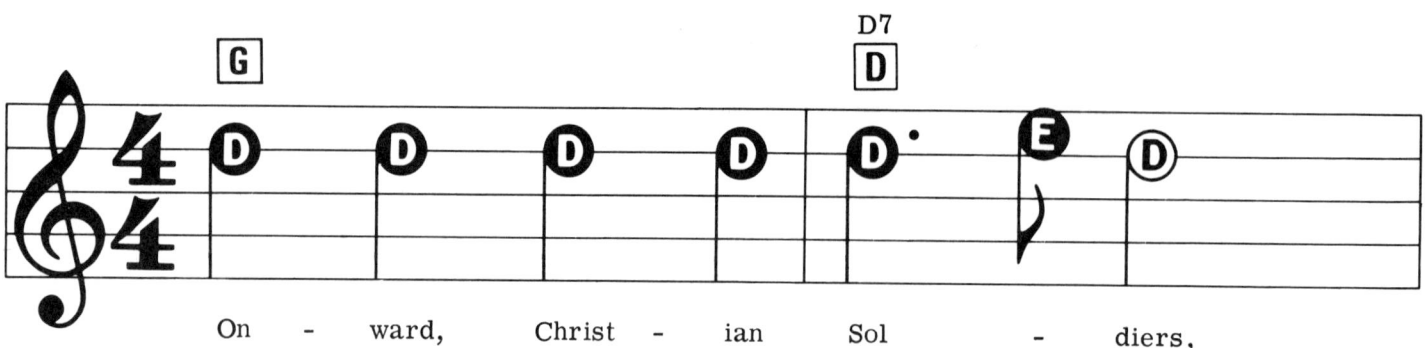

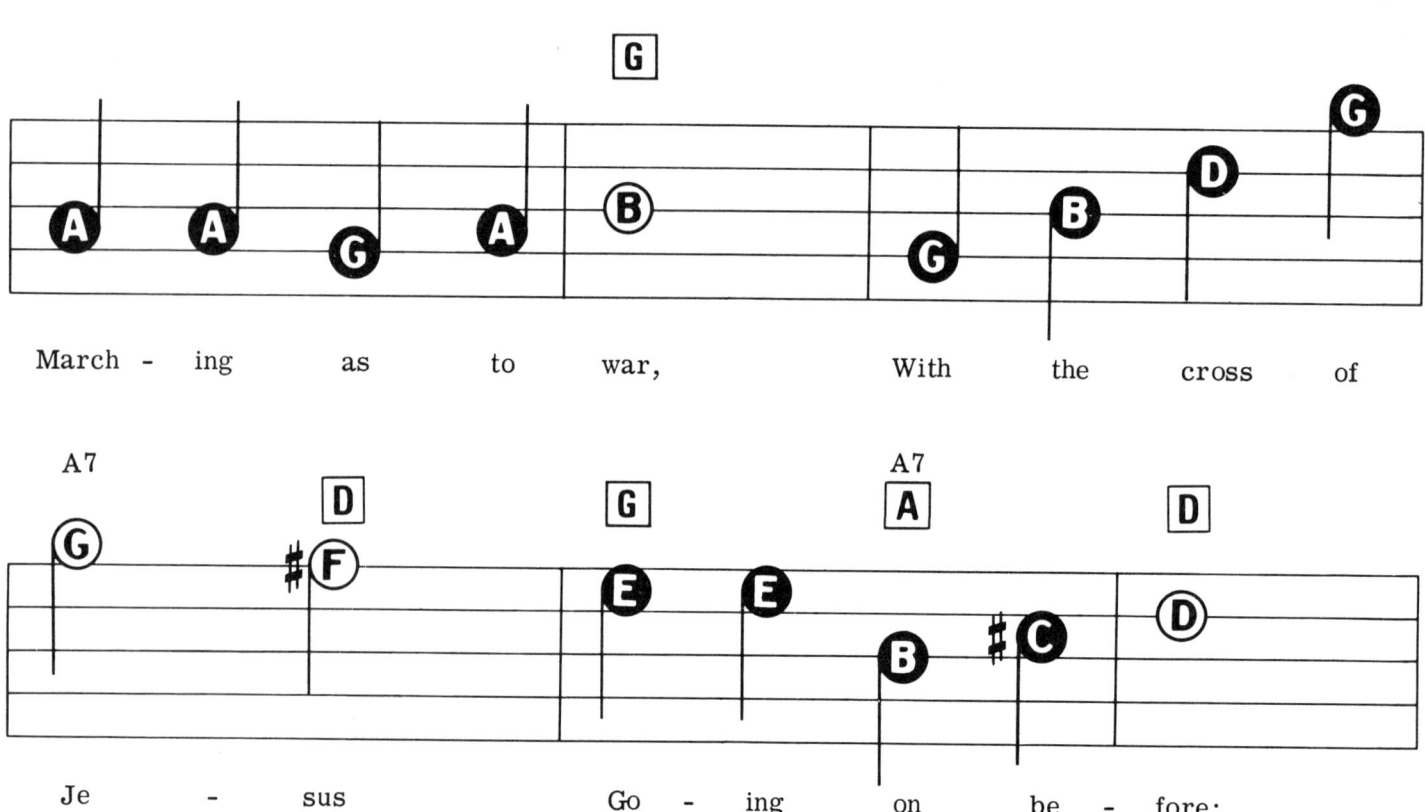

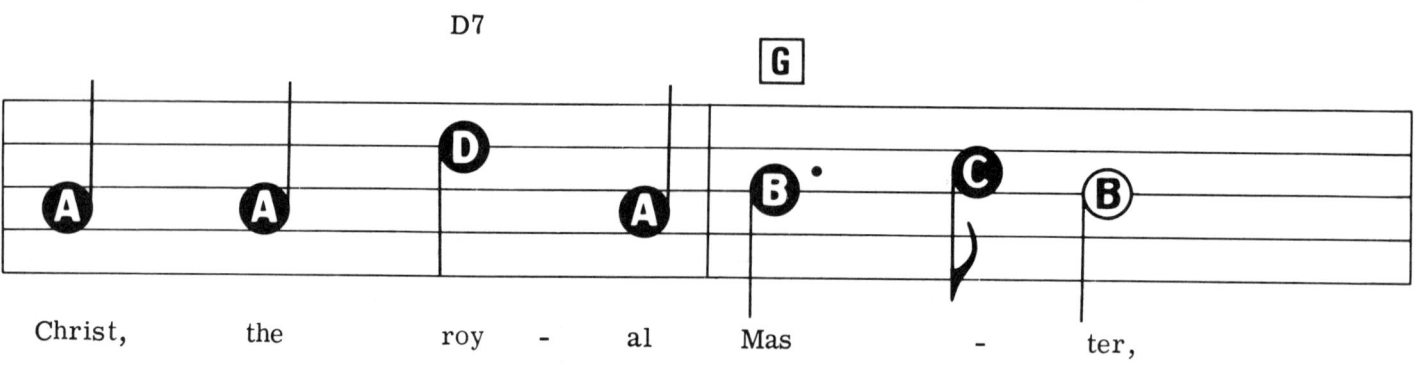

This arr. © Copyright 1975 by HAL LEONARD PUBLISHING CORPORATION, Winona, MN 55987
Made in U.S.A.   International Copyright Secured   All Rights Reserved

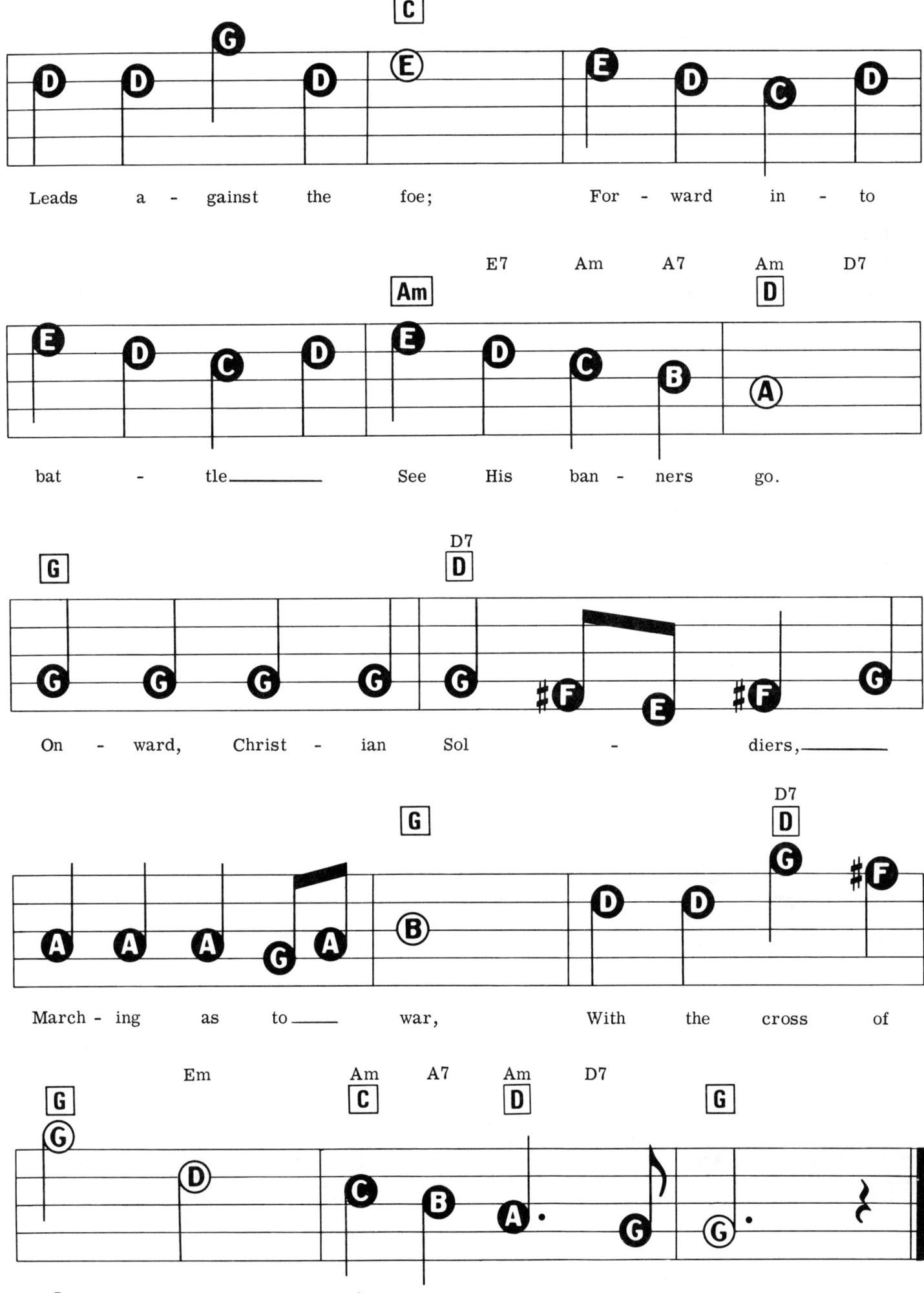

Pass Me Not, O Gentle Saviour

Registration 1
Rhythm: March

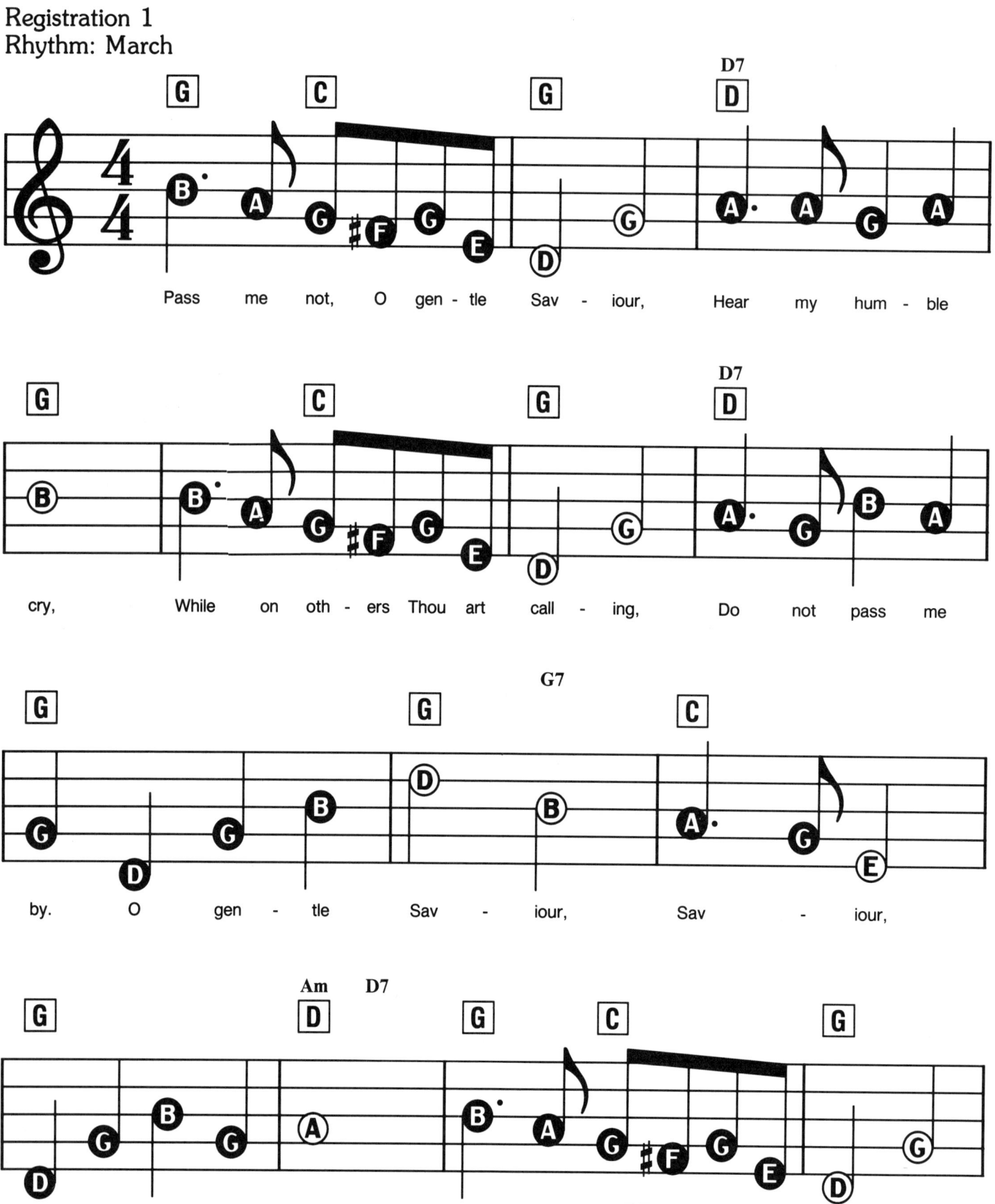

Copyright © 1991 by HAL LEONARD PUBLISHING CORPORATION
International Copyright Secured   All Rights Reserved

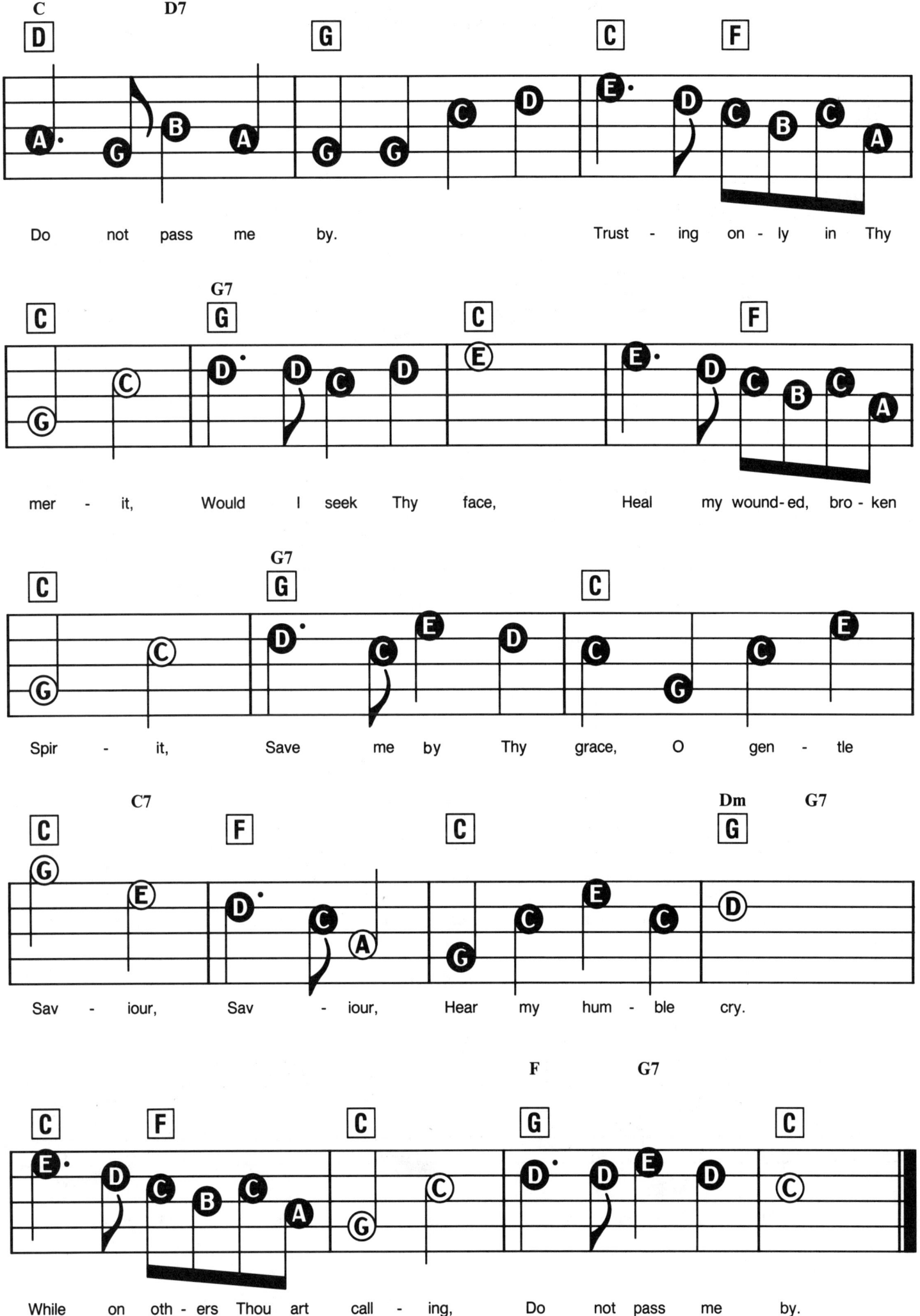

Rock Of Ages

Registration 6

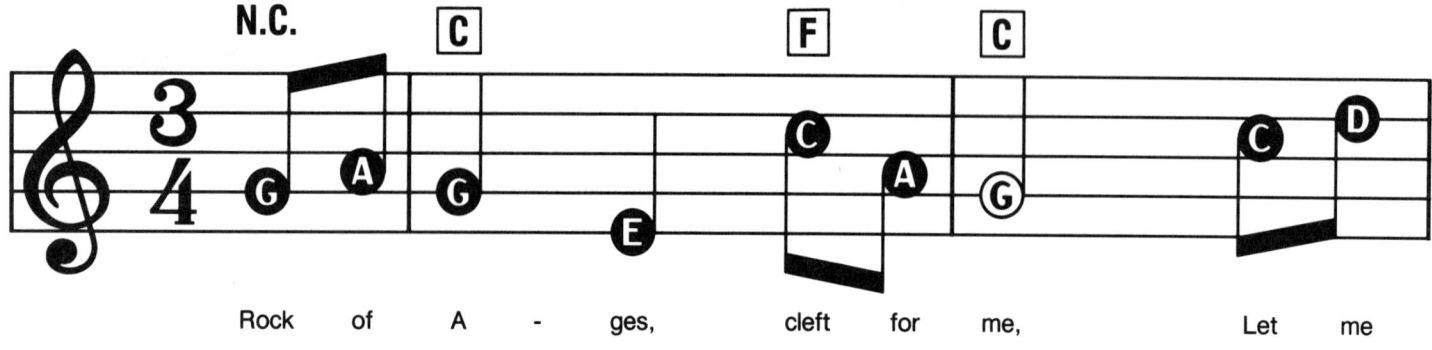

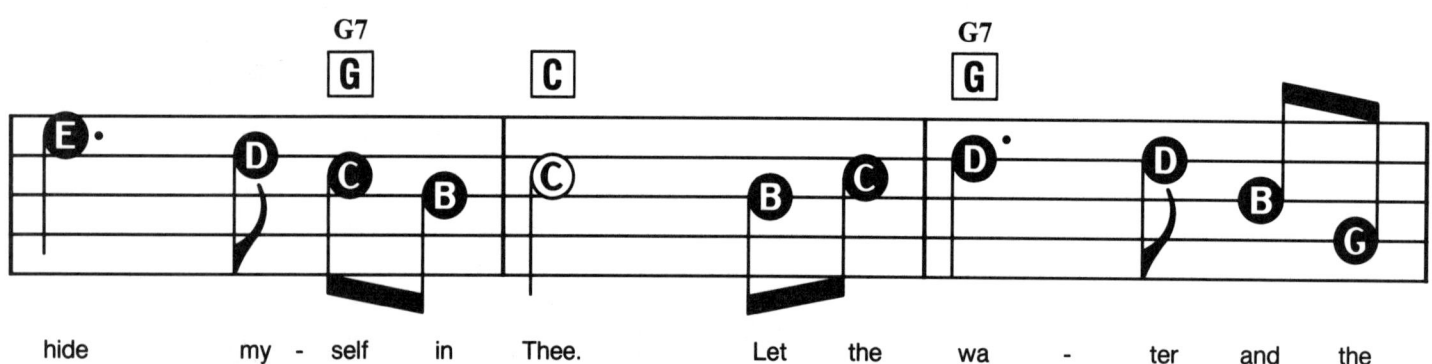

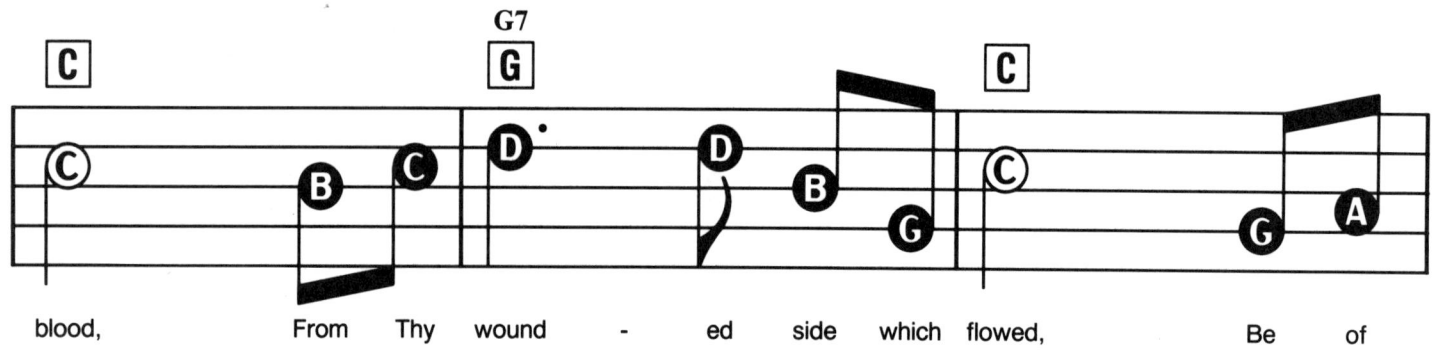

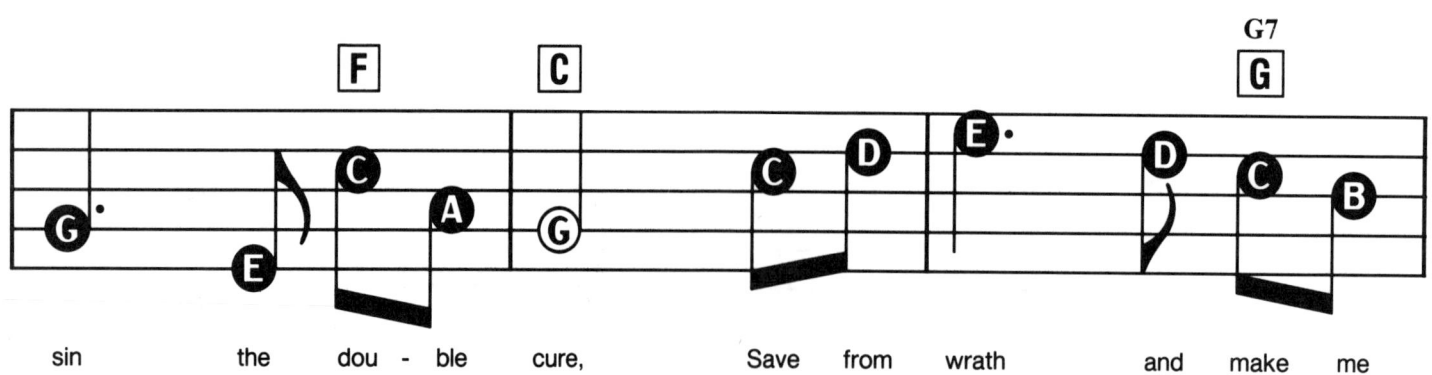

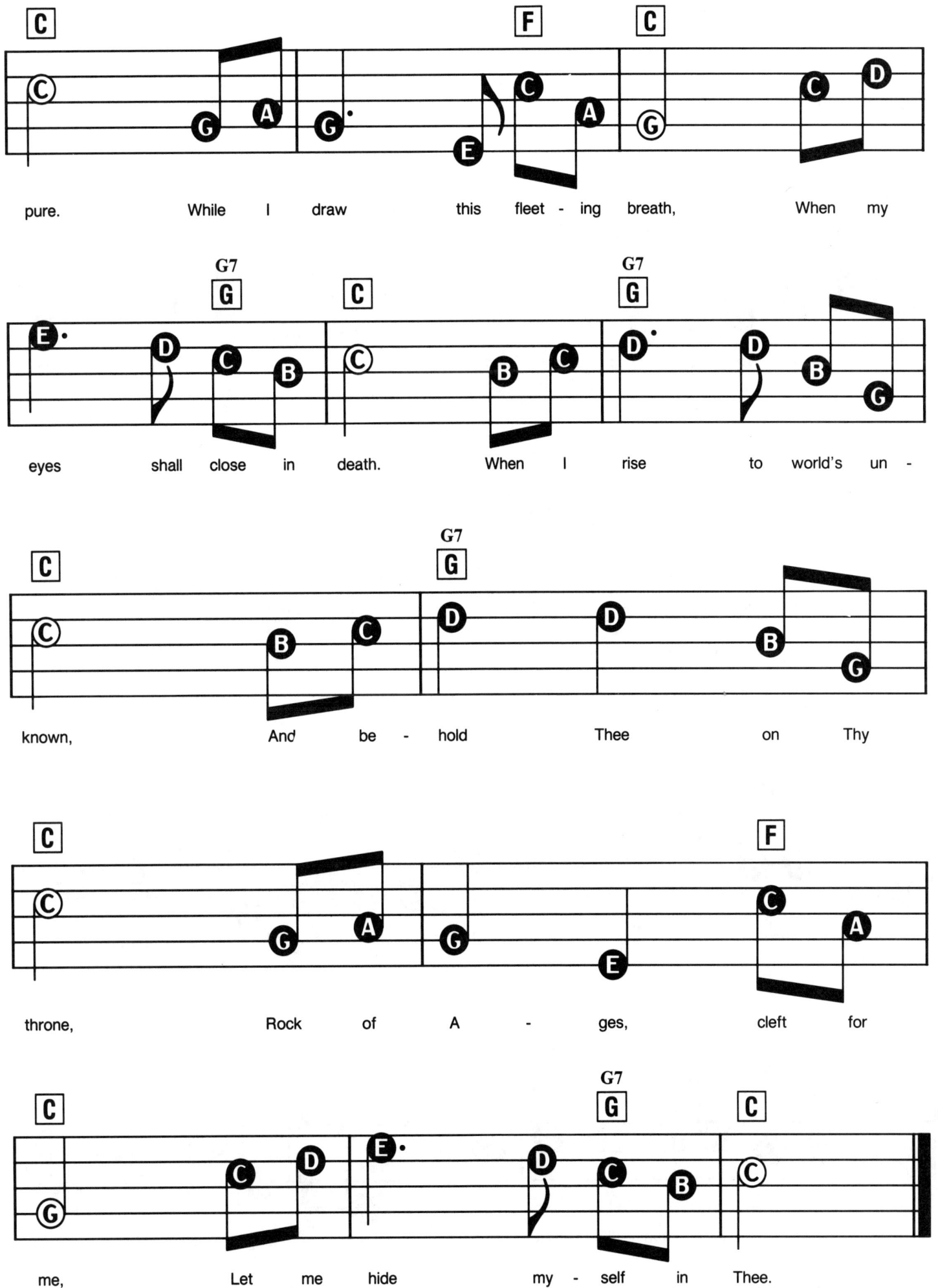

Saviour, Like A Shepherd Lead Us

Registration 4

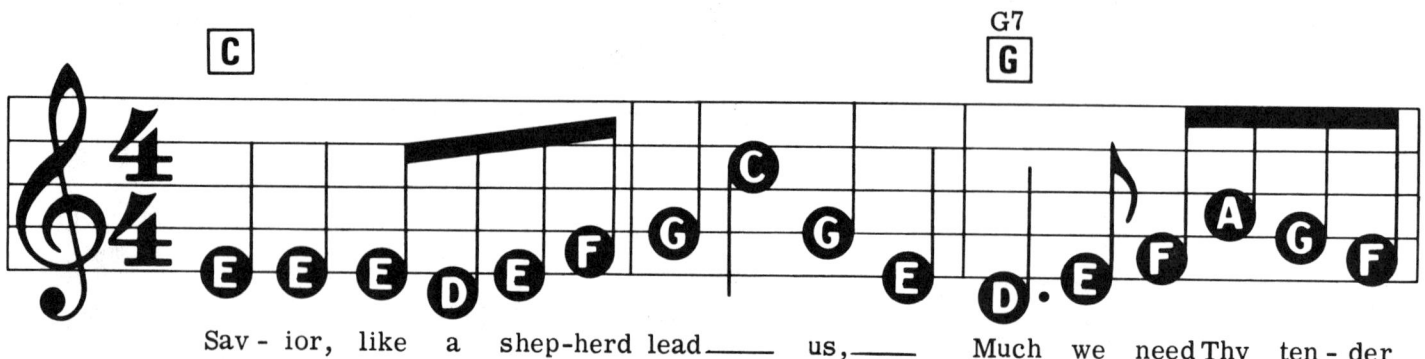
Sav-ior, like a shep-herd lead us, Much we need Thy ten-der

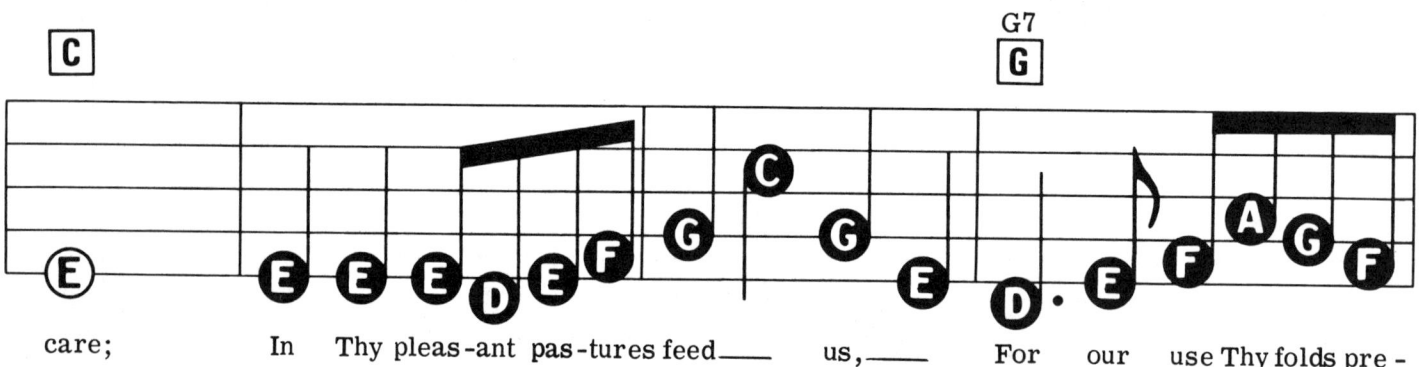
care; In Thy pleas-ant pas-tures feed us, For our use Thy folds pre-

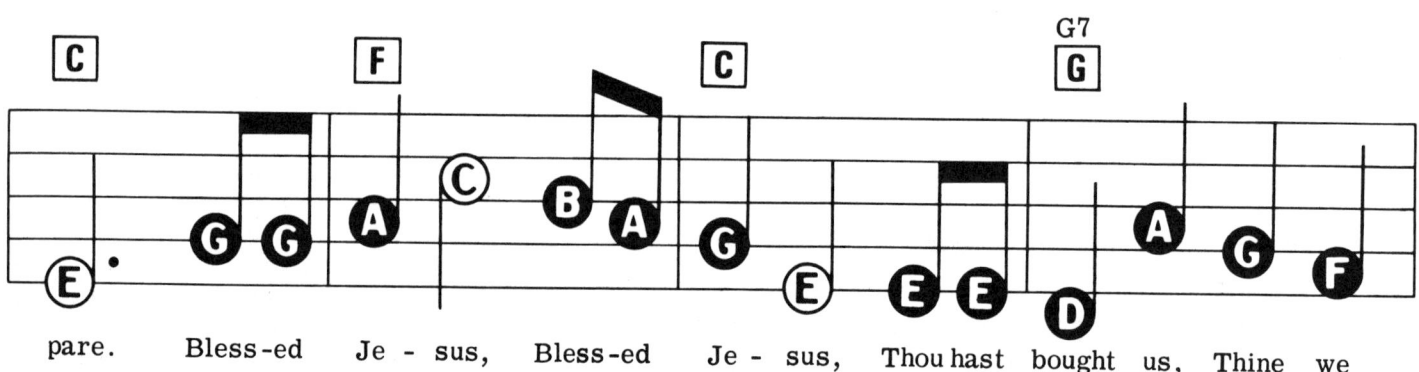
pare. Bless-ed Je-sus, Bless-ed Je-sus, Thou hast bought us, Thine we

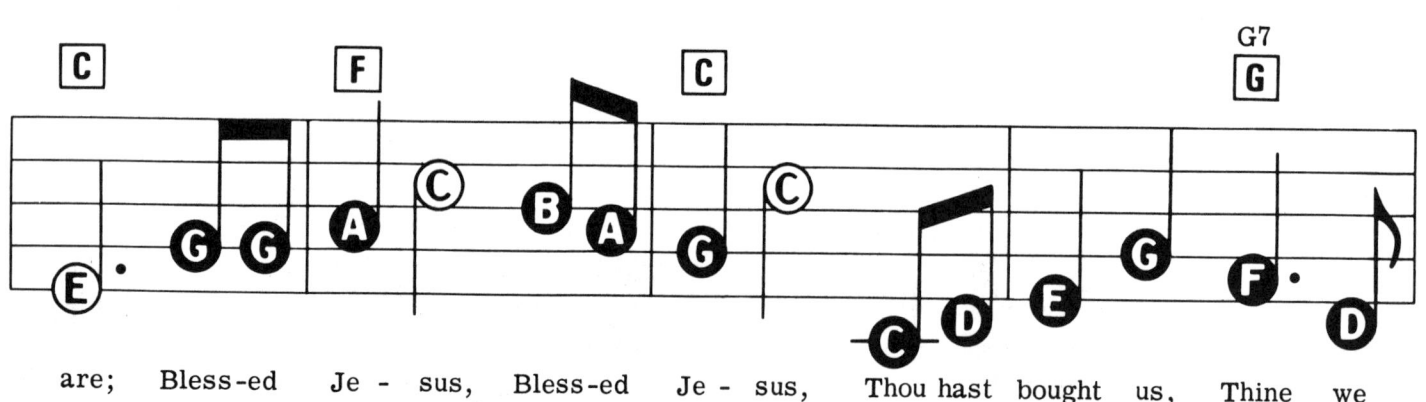
are; Bless-ed Je-sus, Bless-ed Je-sus, Thou hast bought us, Thine we

This arr. © Copyright 1975 by HAL LEONARD PUBLISHING CORPORATION, Winona, MN 55987
Made in U.S.A.   International Copyright Secured   All Rights Reserved

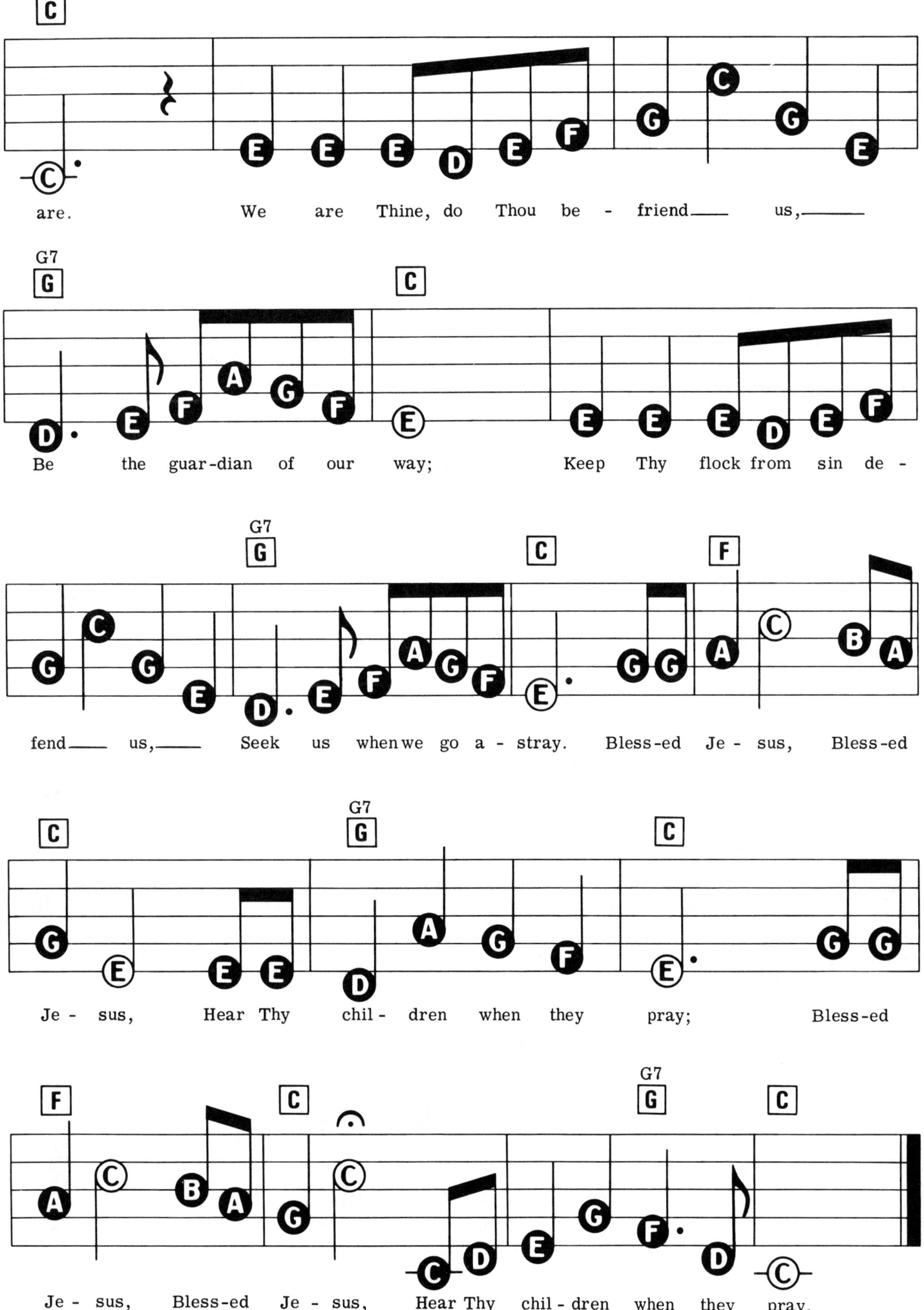

Shall We Gather At The River?

Registration 6
Rhythm: March

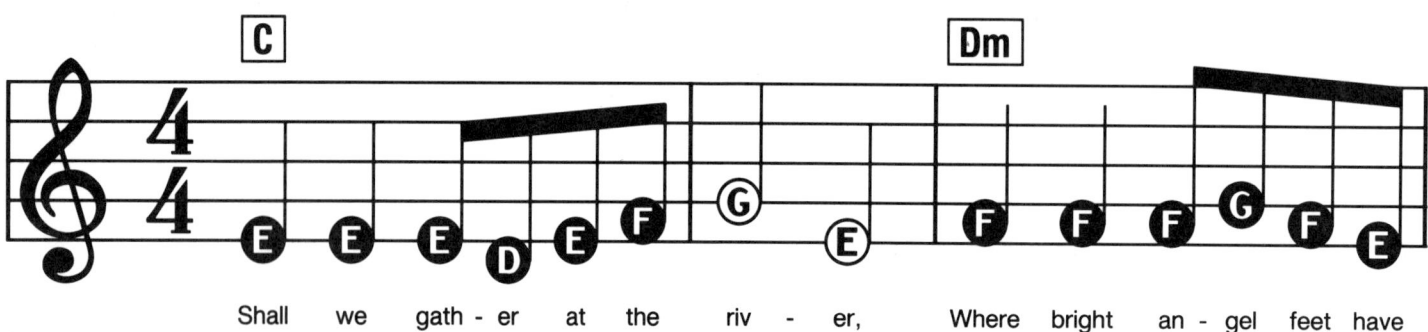
Shall we gath-er at the riv-er, Where bright an-gel feet have

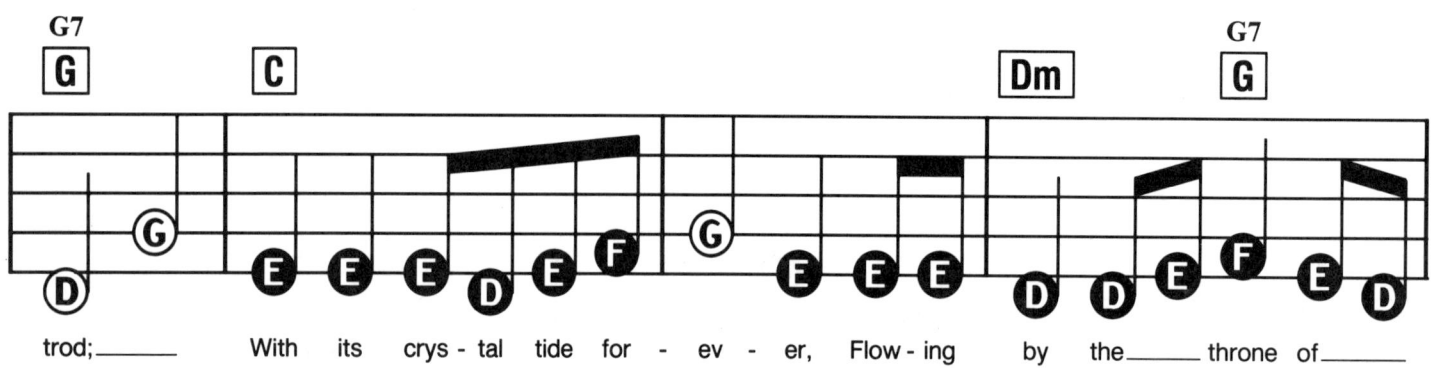
trod;___ With its crys-tal tide for-ev-er, Flow-ing by the___ throne of___

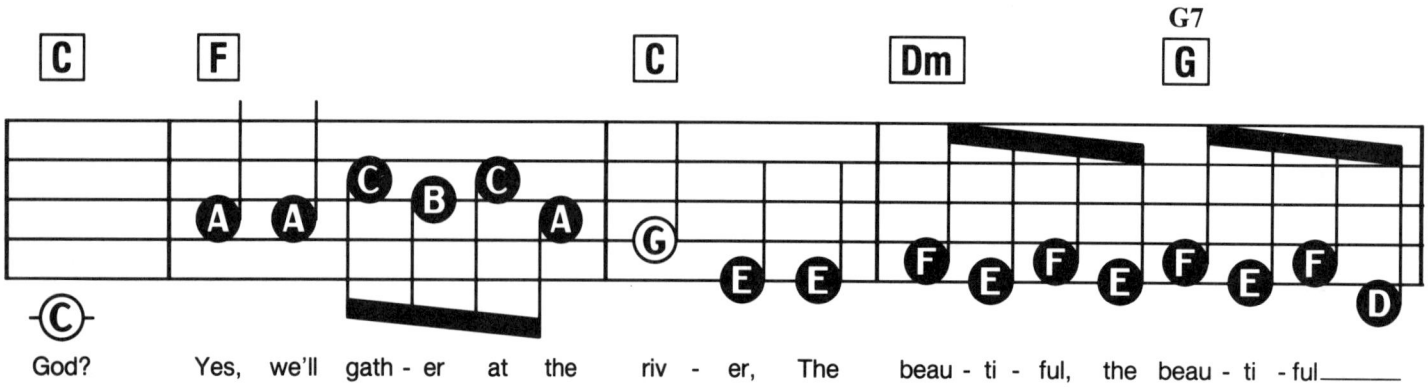
God? Yes, we'll gath-er at the riv-er, The beau-ti-ful, the beau-ti-ful___

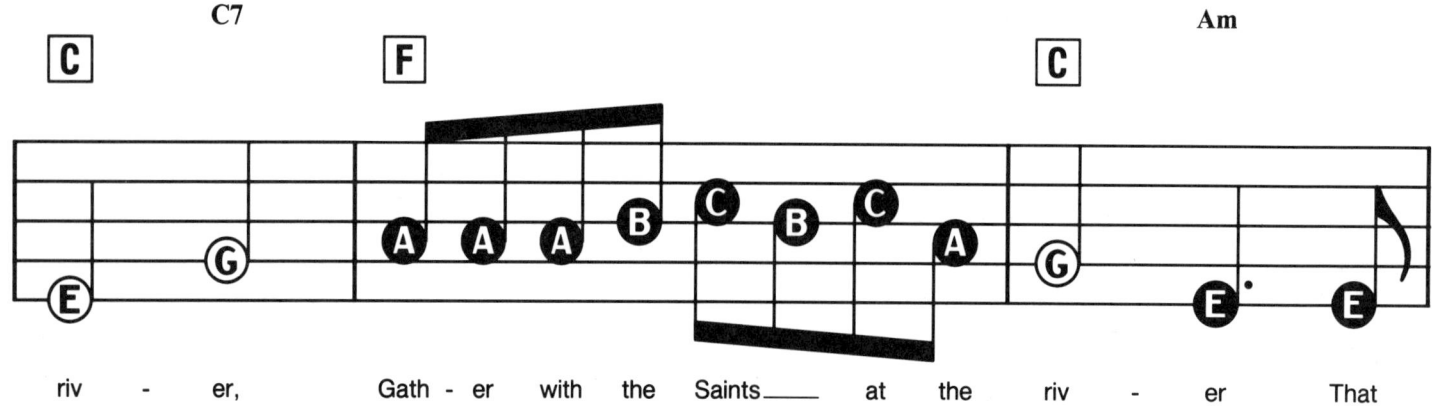
riv-er, Gath-er with the Saints___ at the riv-er That

Copyright © 1991 by HAL LEONARD PUBLISHING CORPORATION
International Copyright Secured   All Rights Reserved

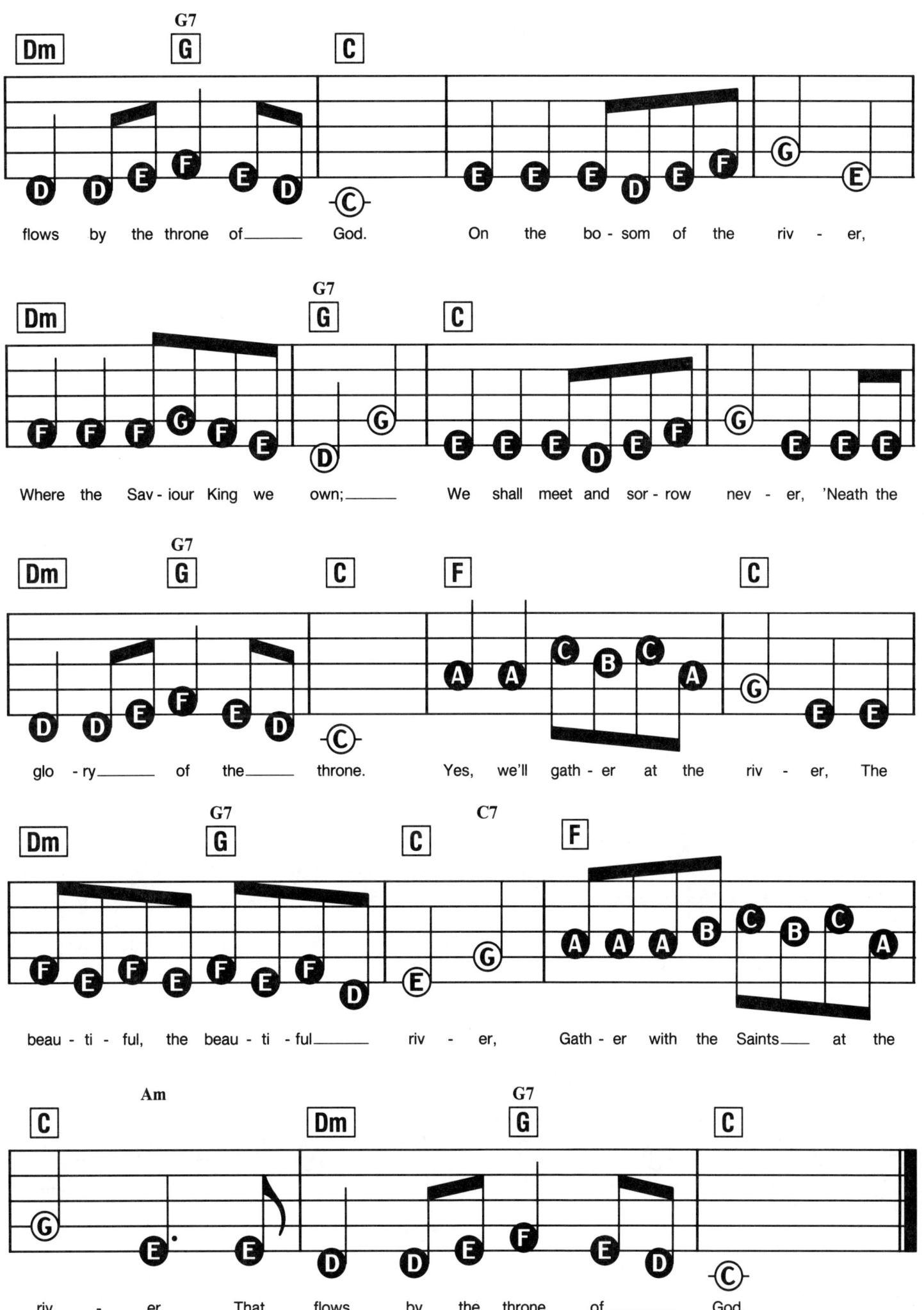

Softly And Tenderly

Registration 2
Rhythm: Waltz

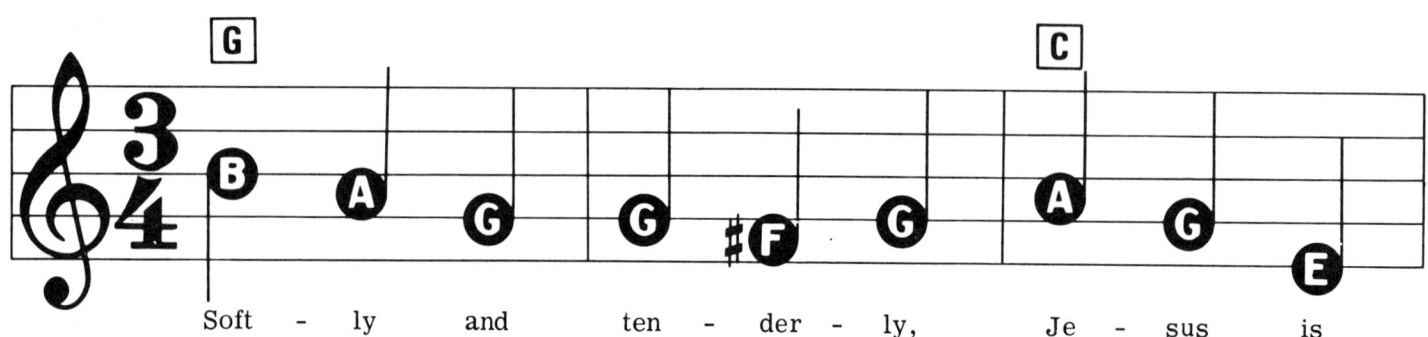
Soft - ly and ten - der - ly, Je - sus is

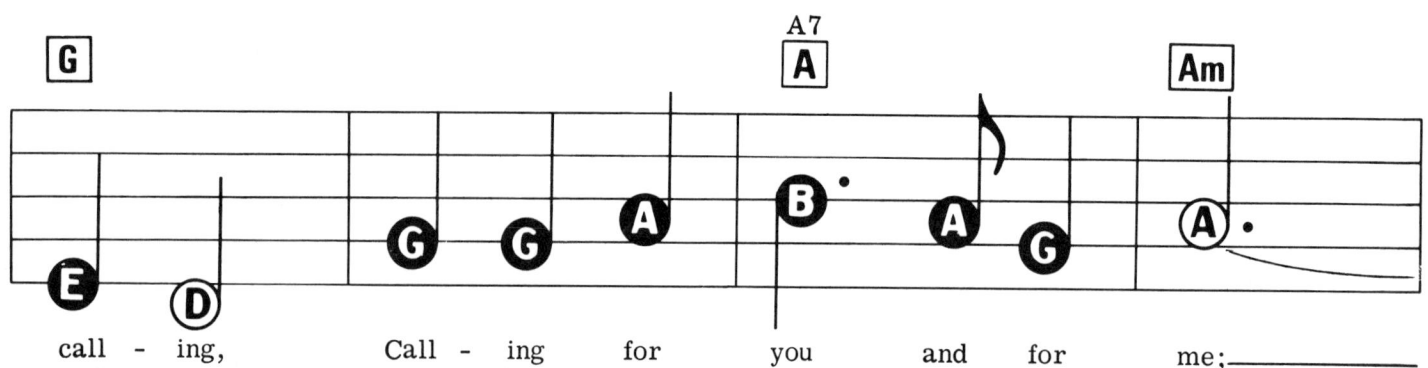
call - ing, Call - ing for you and for me;

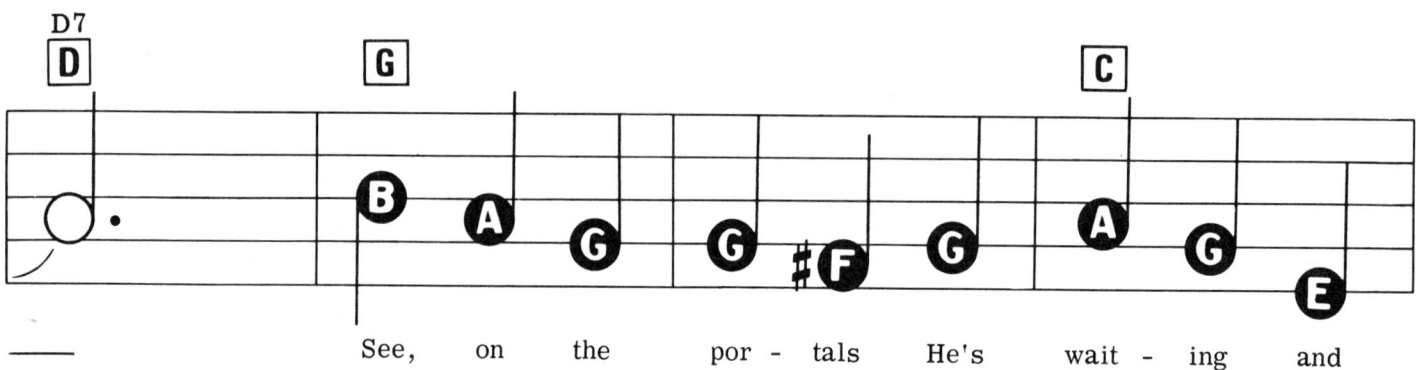
See, on the por - tals He's wait - ing and

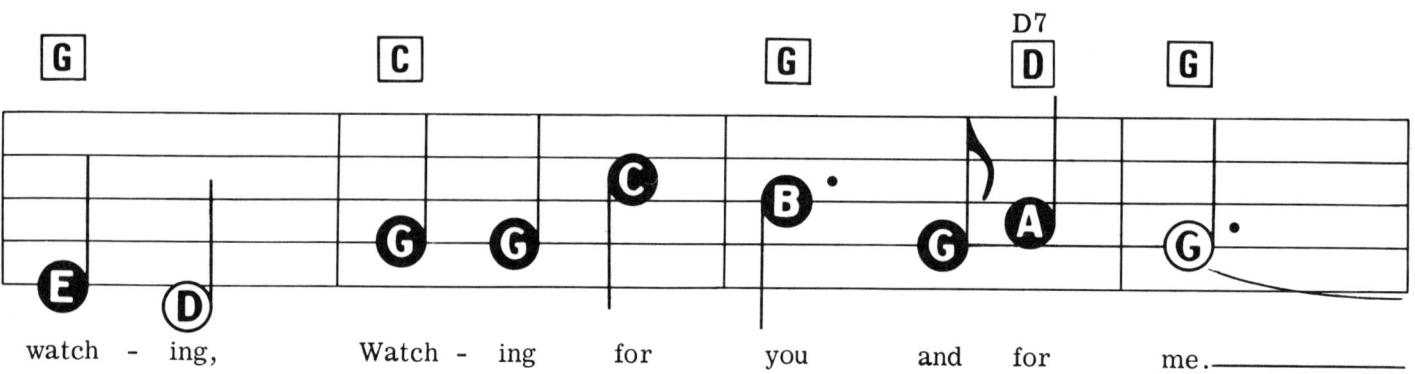
watch - ing, Watch - ing for you and for me.

This arr. © Copyright 1975 by HAL LEONARD PUBLISHING CORPORATION, Winona, MN 55987
Made in U.S.A.   International Copyright Secured   All Rights Reserved

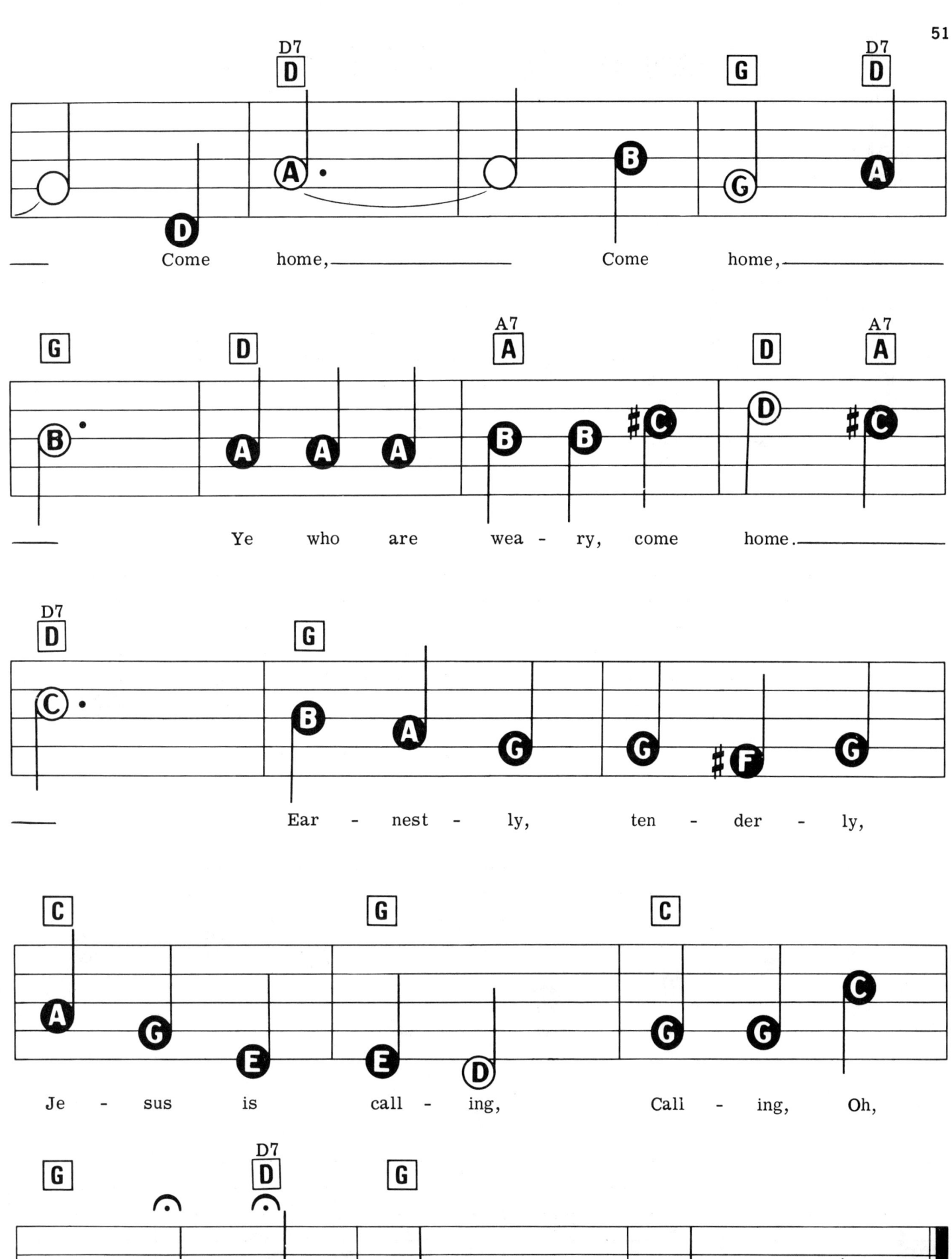

Sweet Hour Of Prayer

Registration 6
Rhythm: Waltz

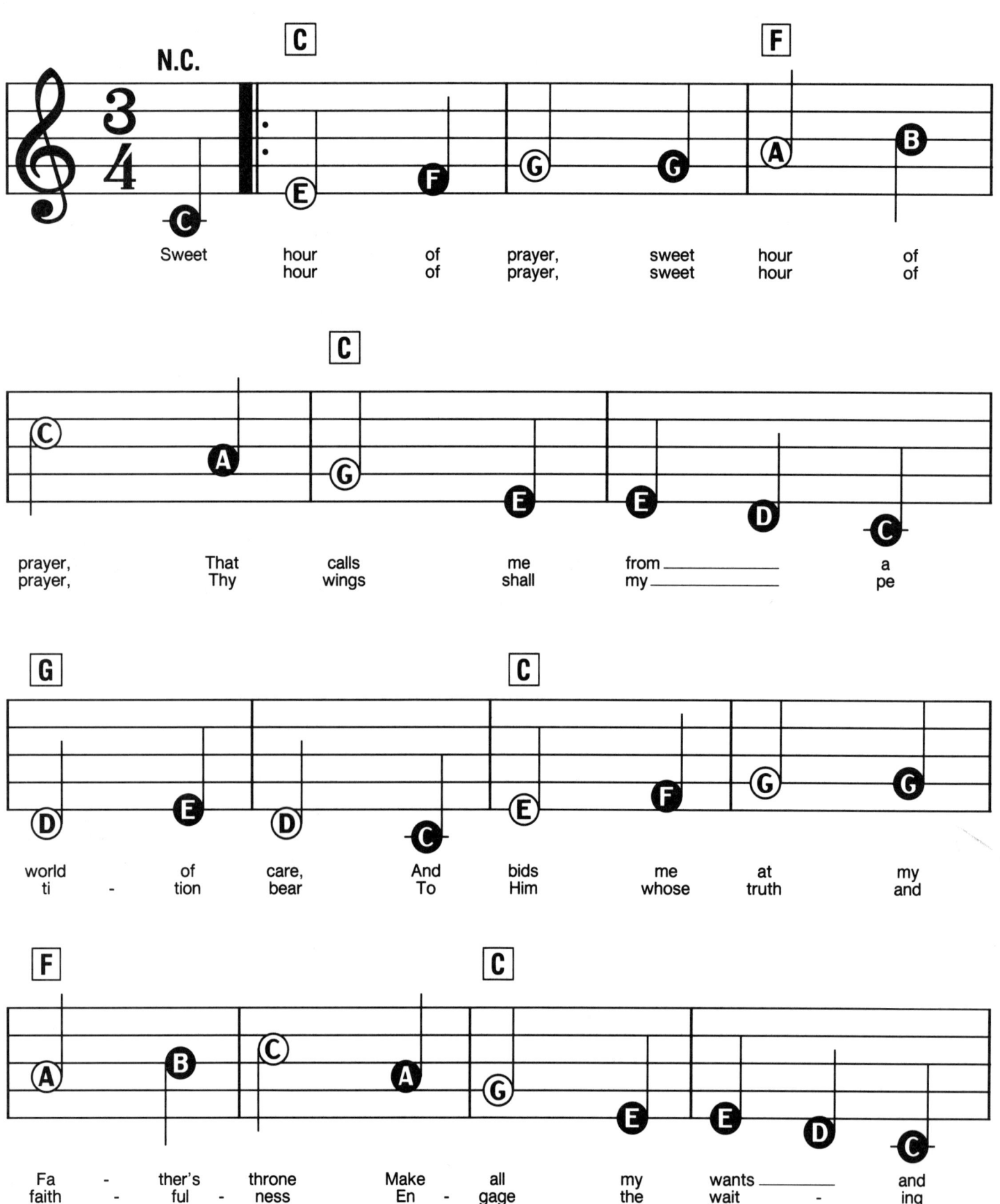

Copyright © 1986 Hal Leonard Publishing Corporation
International Copyright Secured   ALL RIGHTS RESERVED   Printed in the U.S.A.

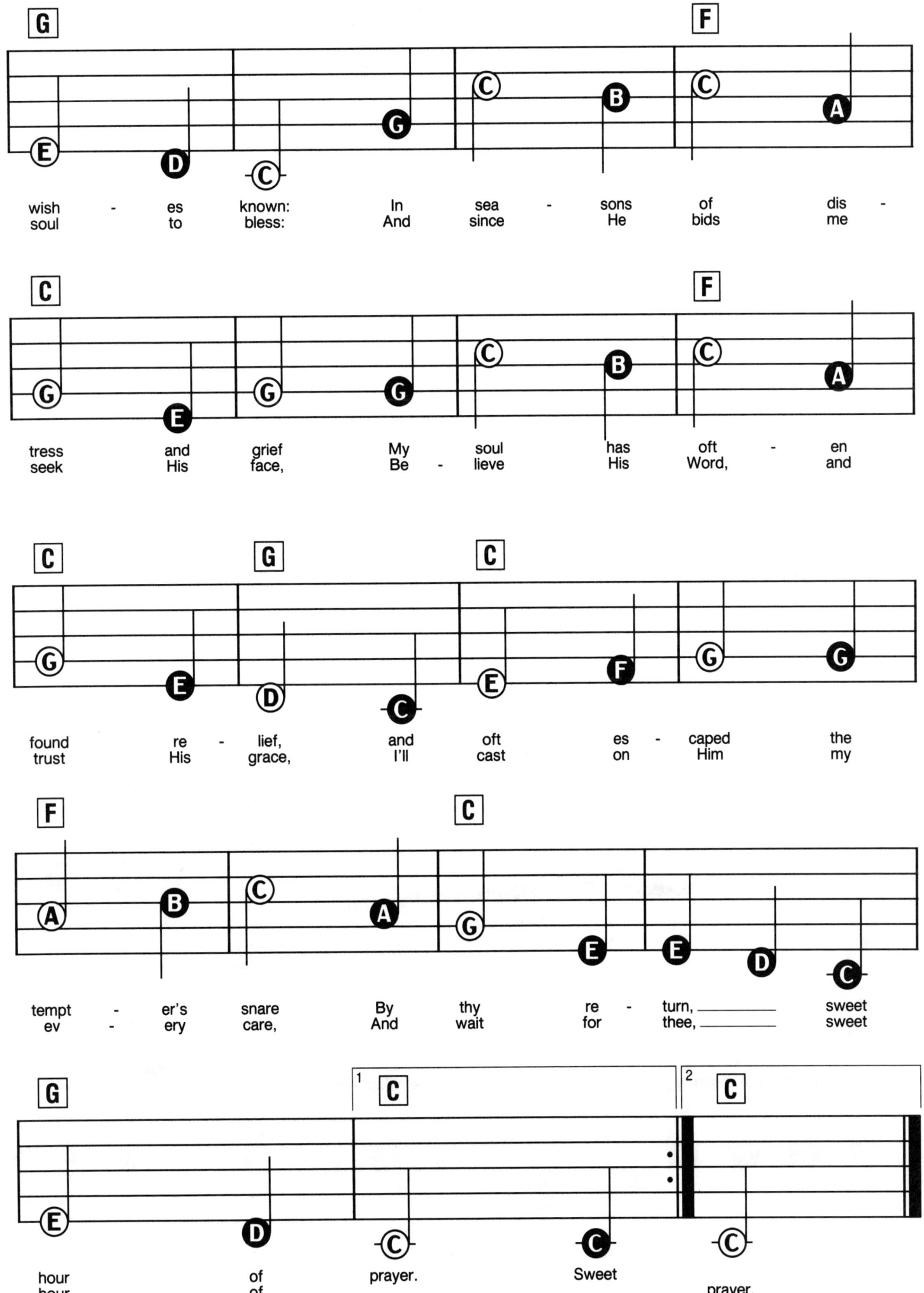

Swing Low, Sweet Chariot

Registration 4
Rhythm: Swing

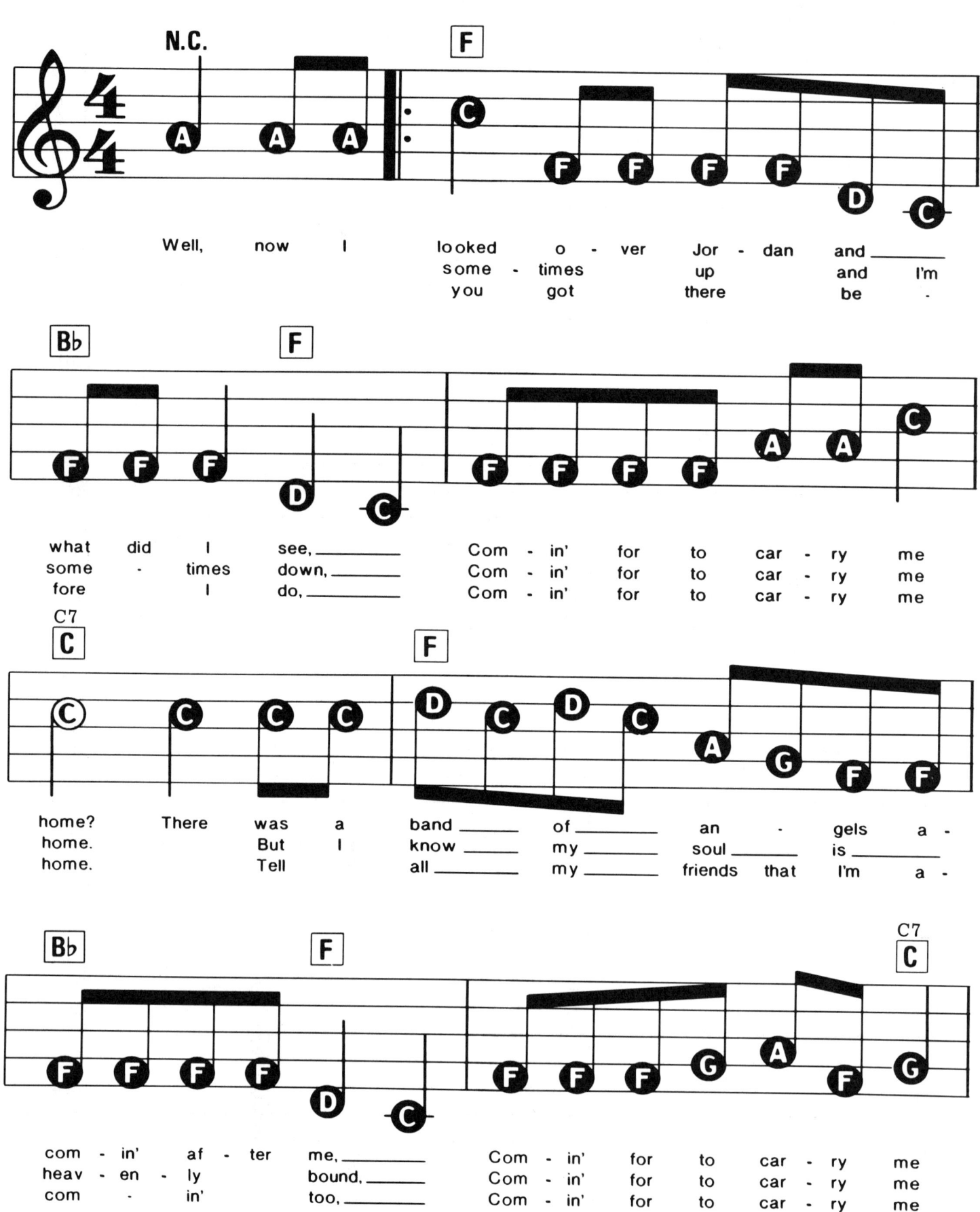

Copyright © 1989 by HAL LEONARD PUBLISHING CORPORATION
International Copyright Secured   ALL RIGHTS RESERVED   Printed in the U.S.A.

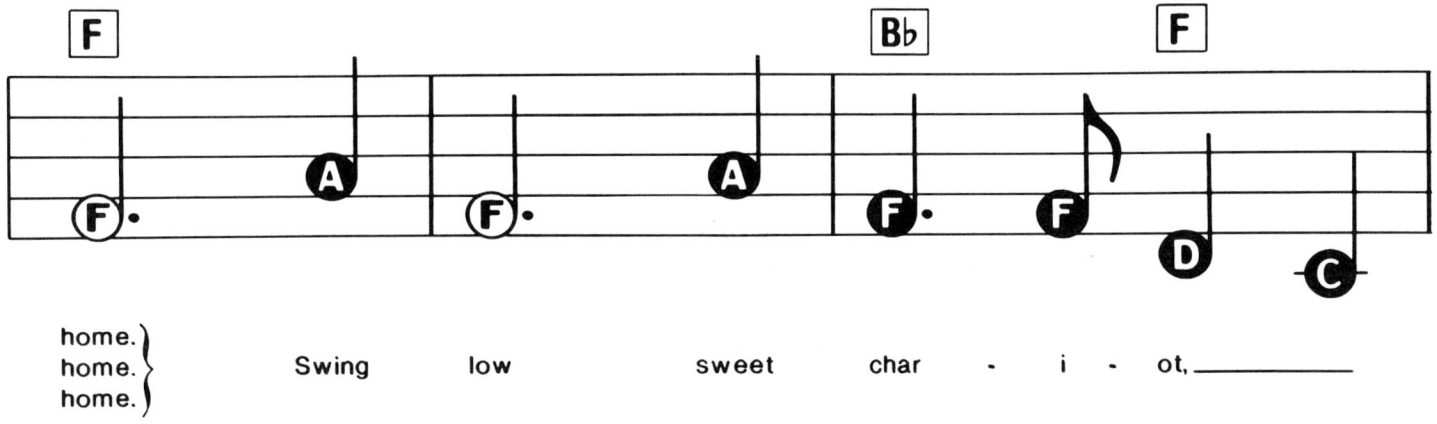
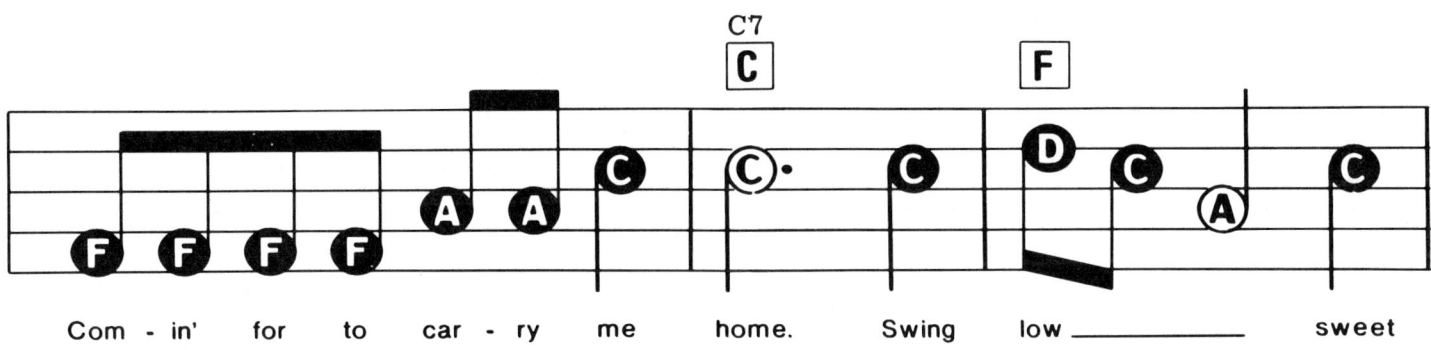
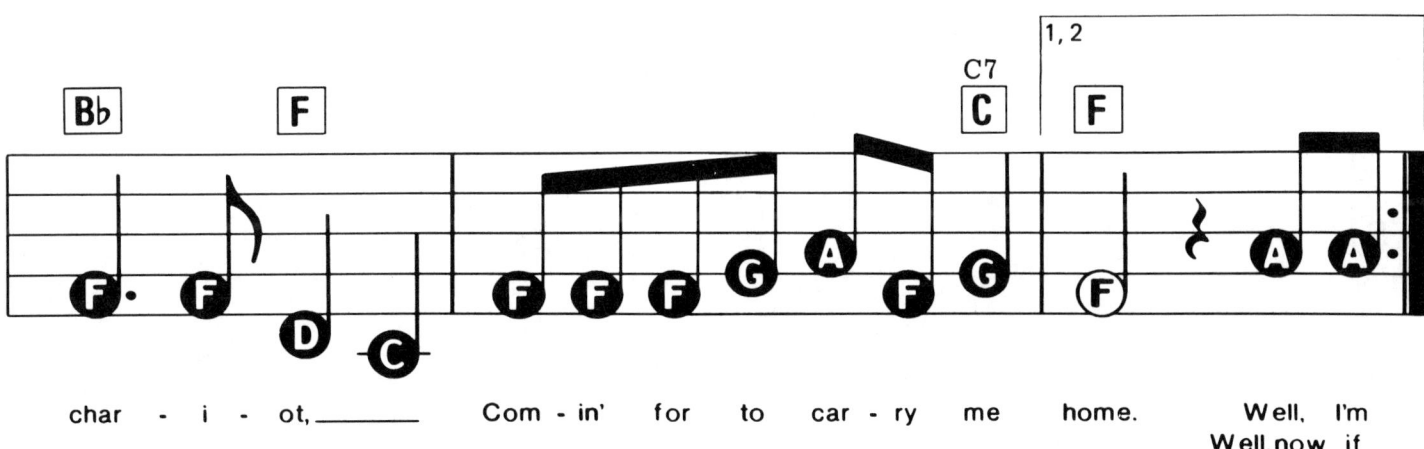
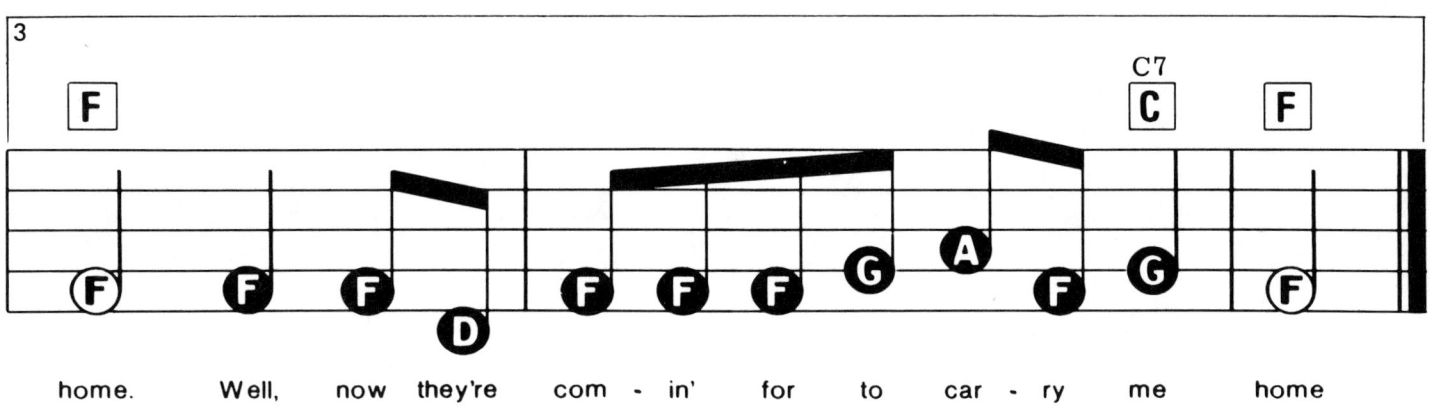

We Gather Together To Ask The Lord's Blessing

Registration 3

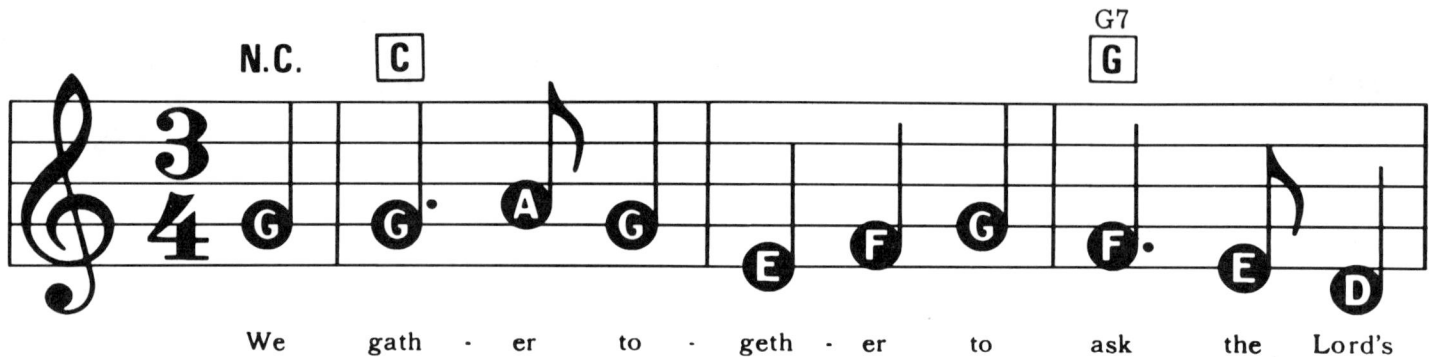
We gath-er to-geth-er to ask the Lord's

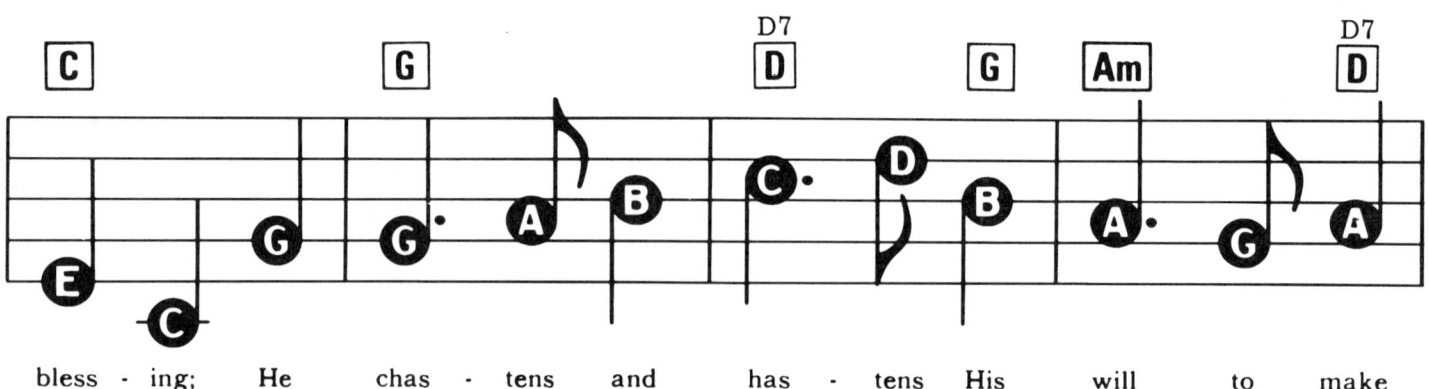
bless-ing; He chas-tens and has-tens His will to make

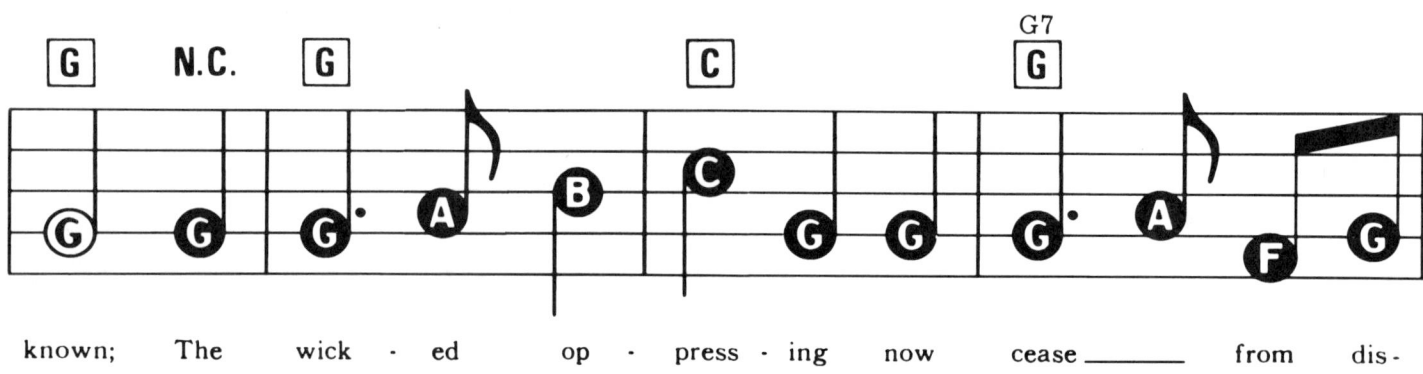
known; The wick-ed op-press-ing now cease____ from dis-

tress-ing; Sing prais-es to His Name:____ He for-

This arrangement © 1979 by HAL LEONARD PUBLISHING CORPORATION
Made in U.S.A.   International Copyright Secured   All Rights Reserved

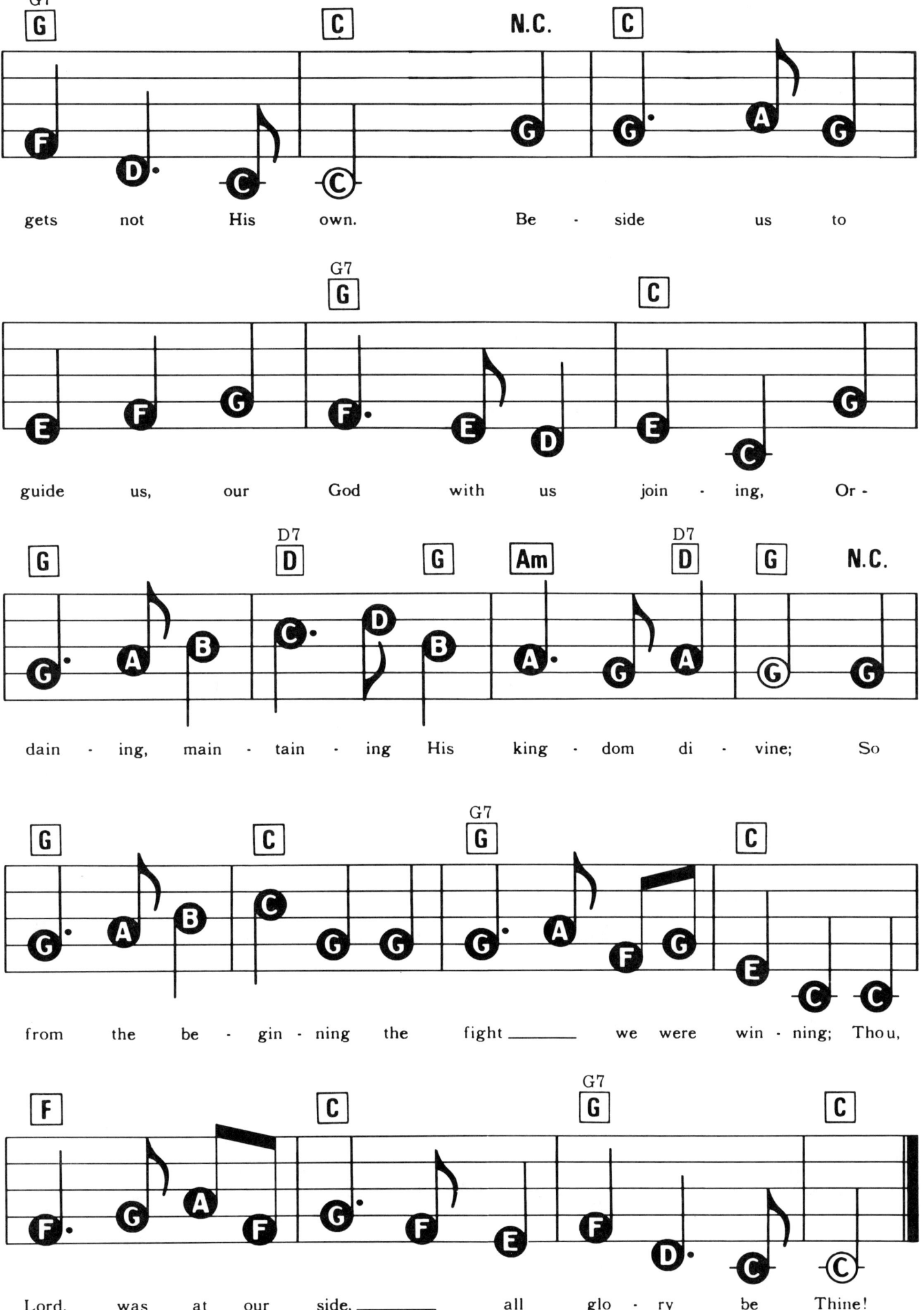

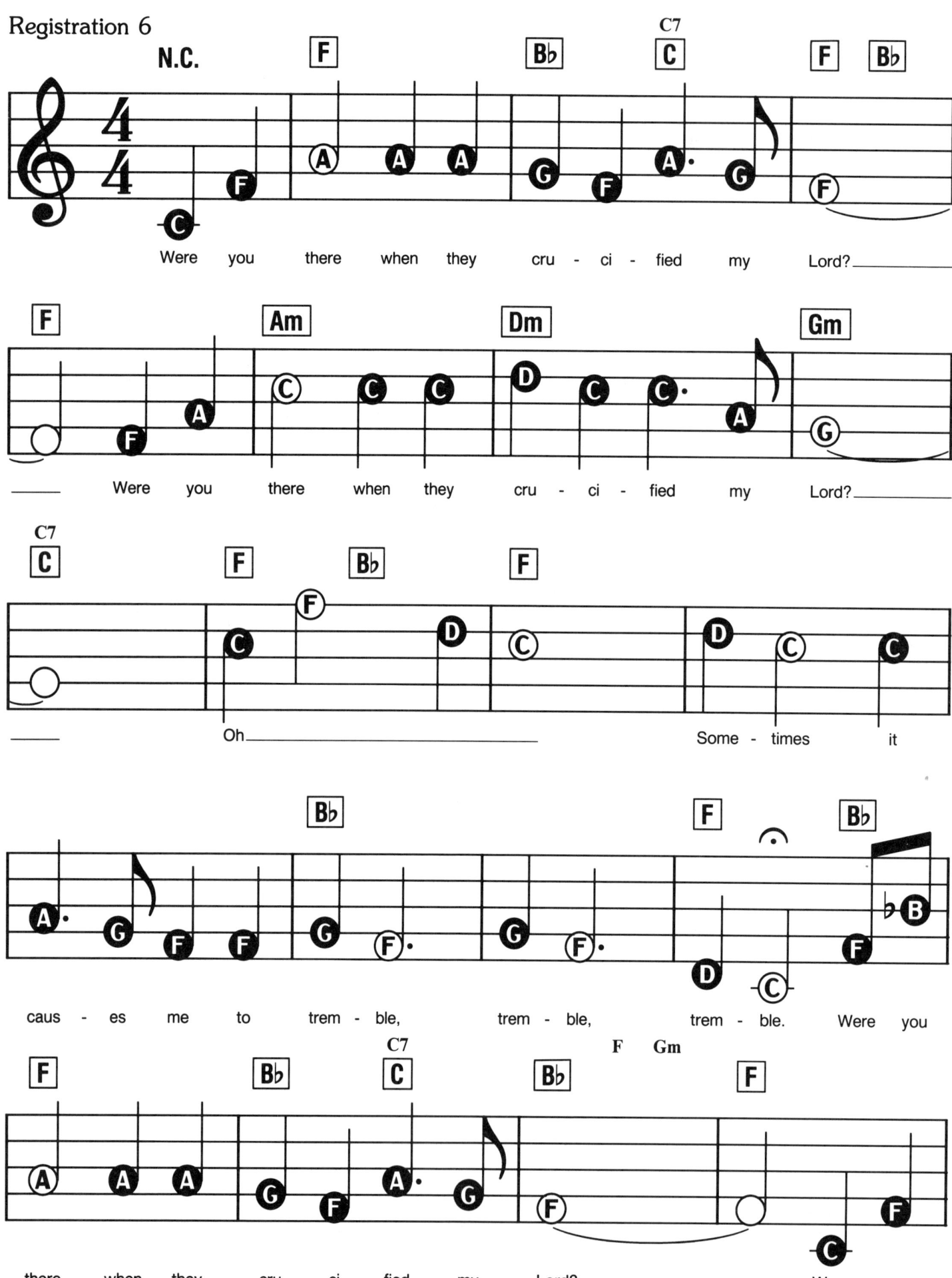

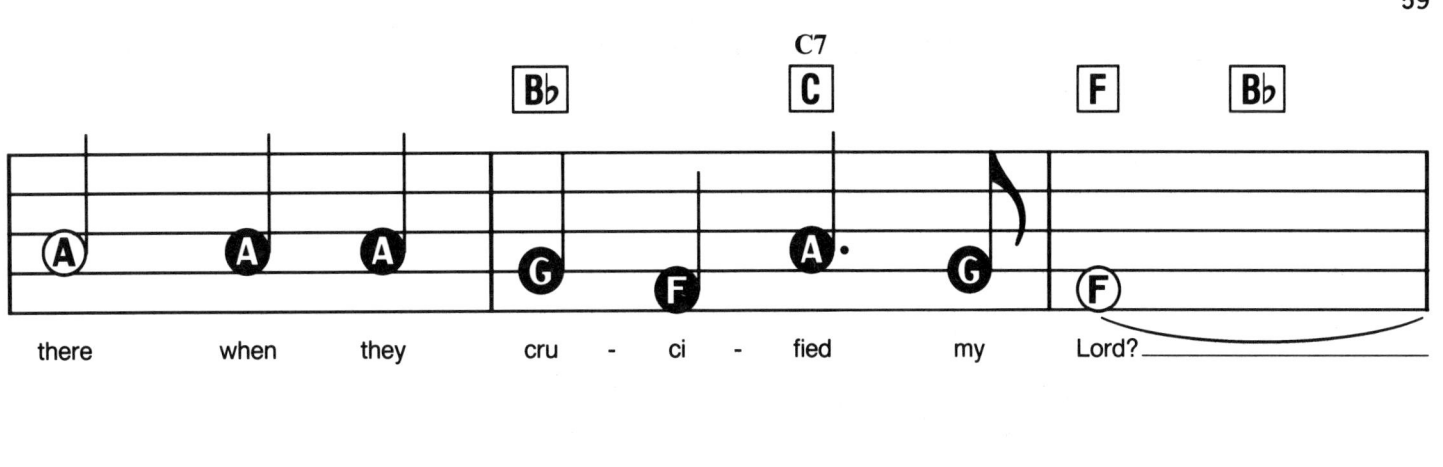
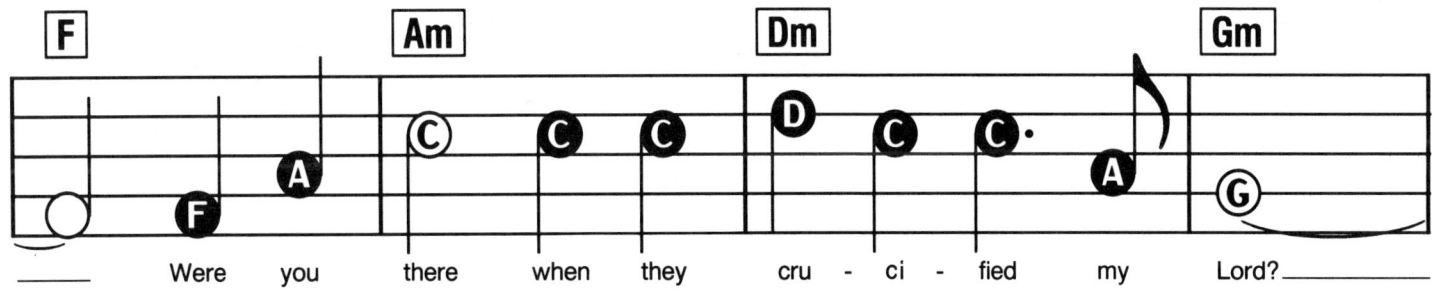
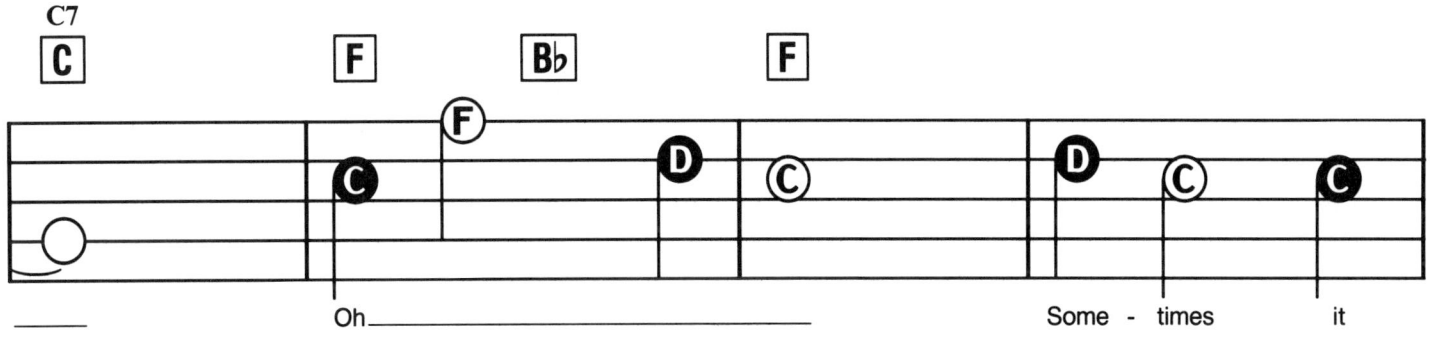
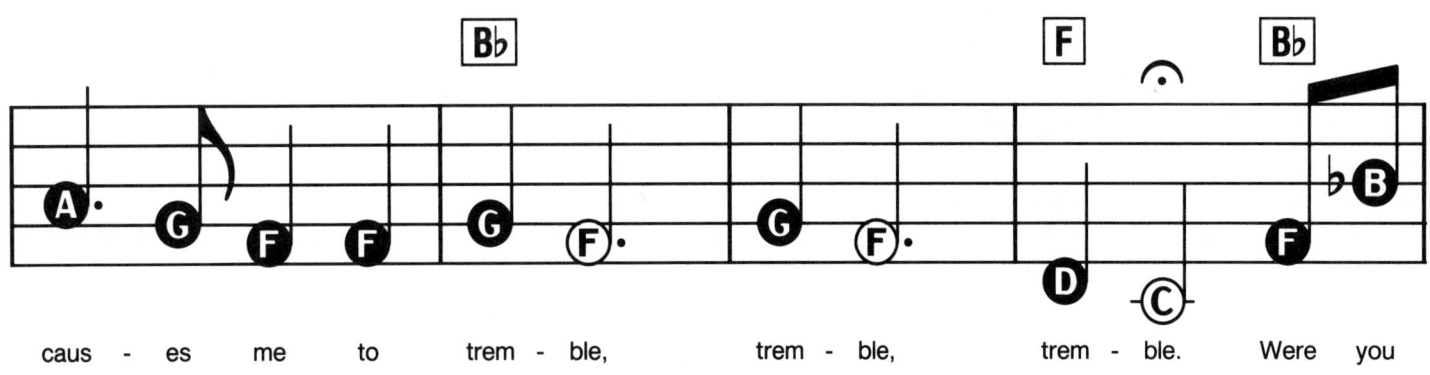
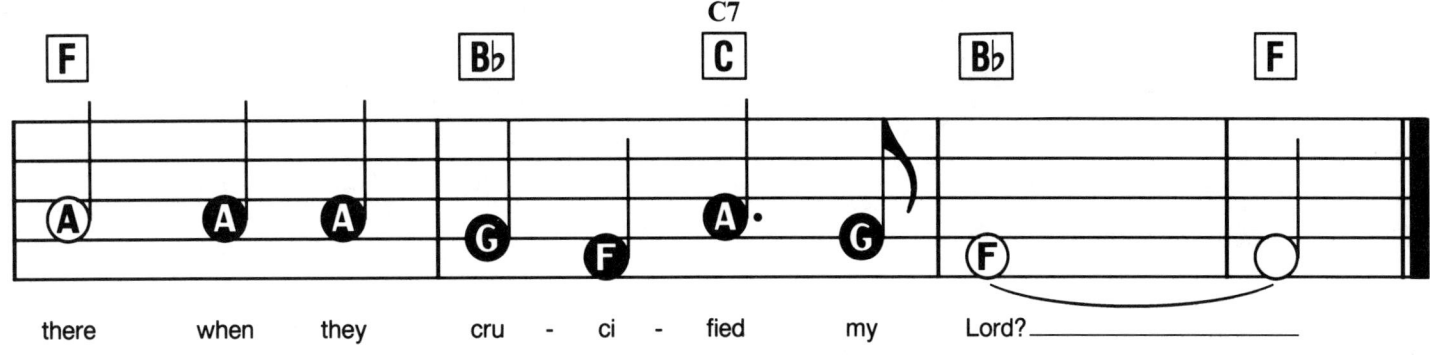

What A Friend We Have In Jesus

Registration 3

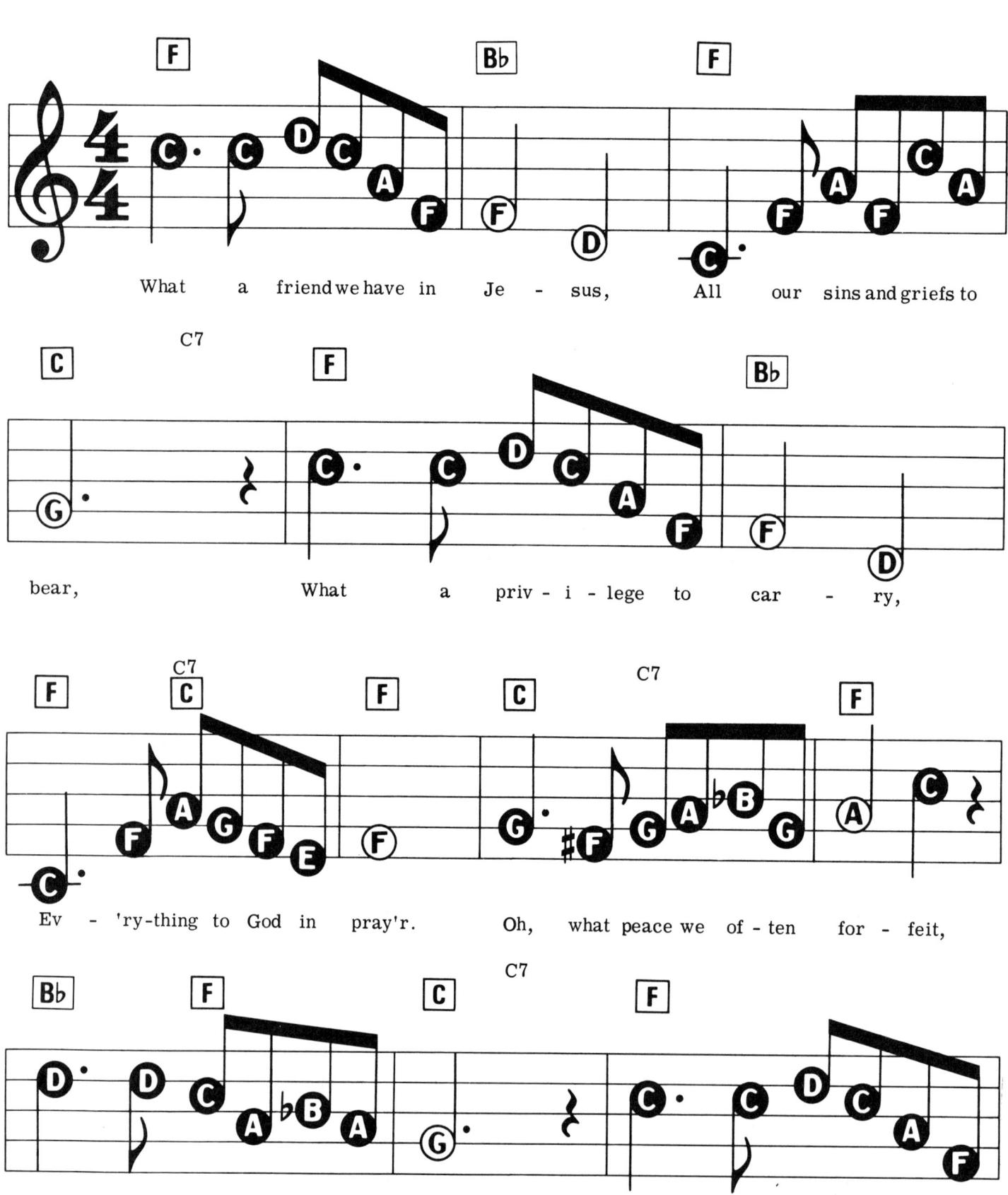

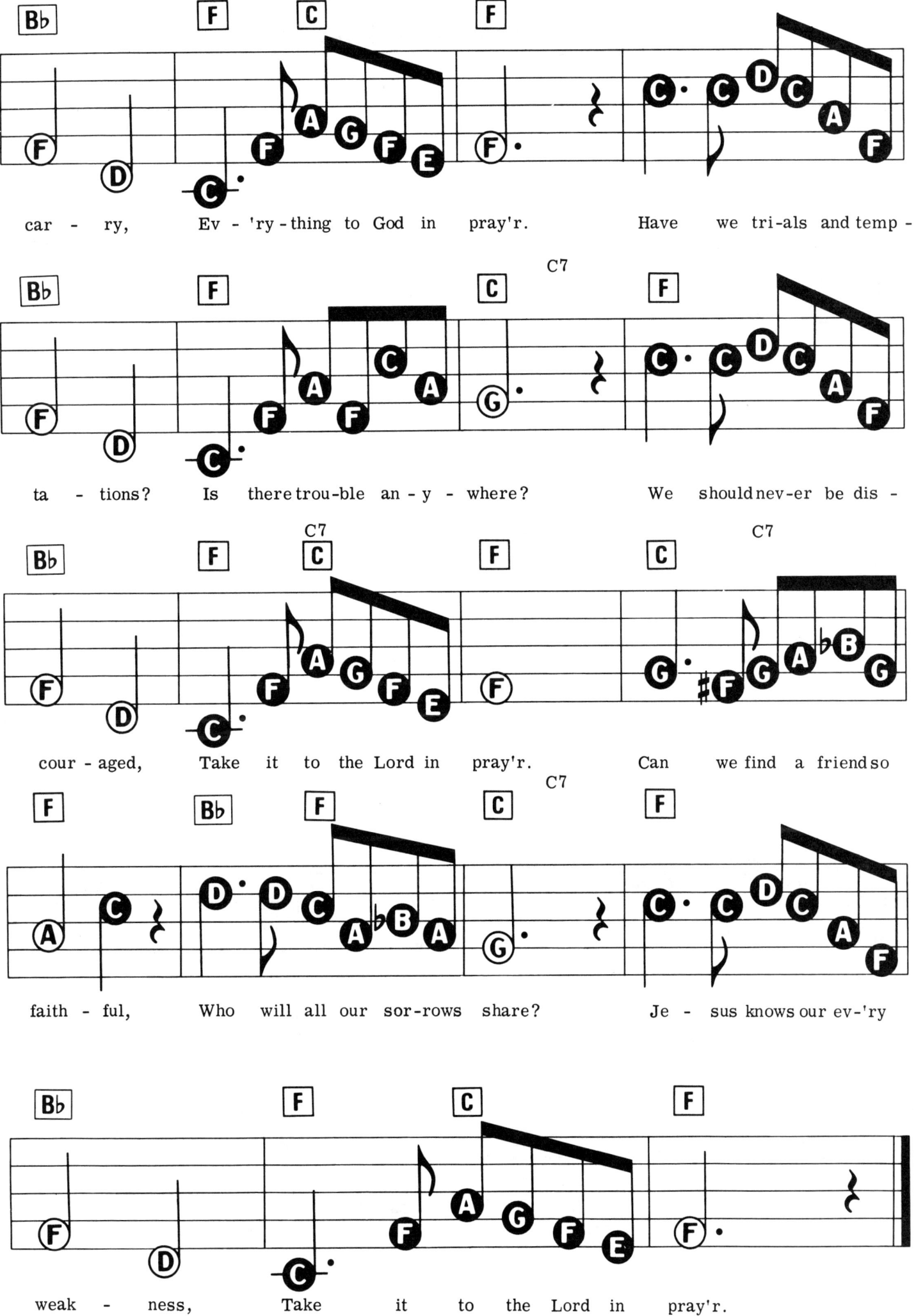

Whispering Hope

Registration 10
Rhythm: Waltz

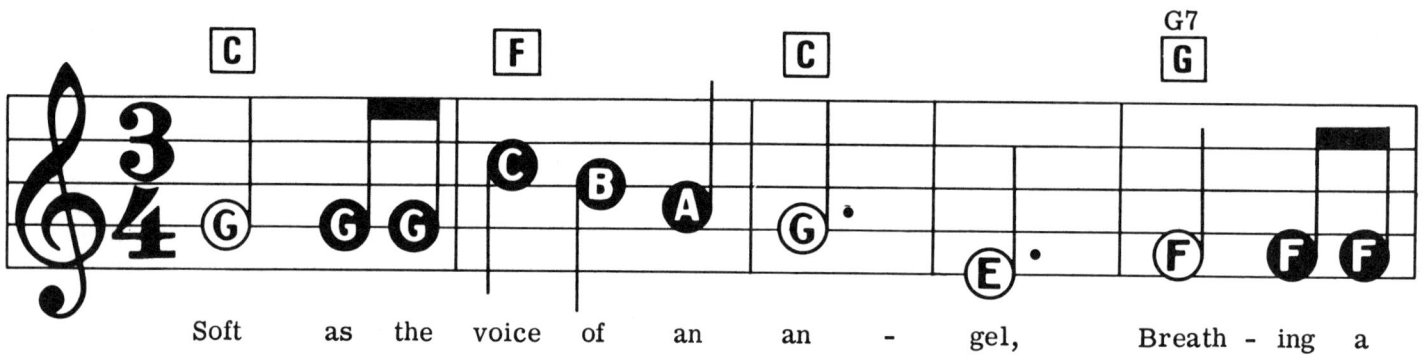
Soft as the voice of an an - gel, Breath - ing a

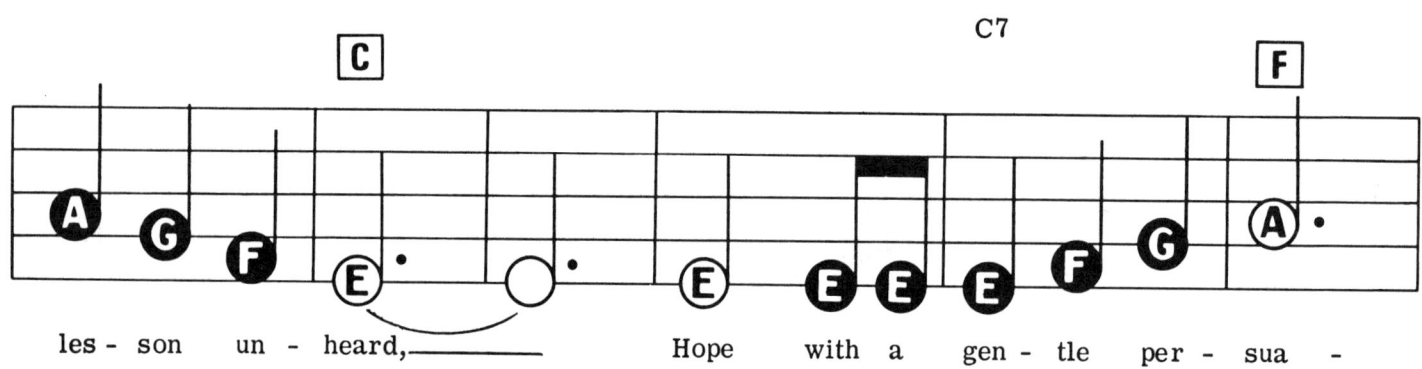
les - son un - heard,_____ Hope with a gen - tle per - sua -

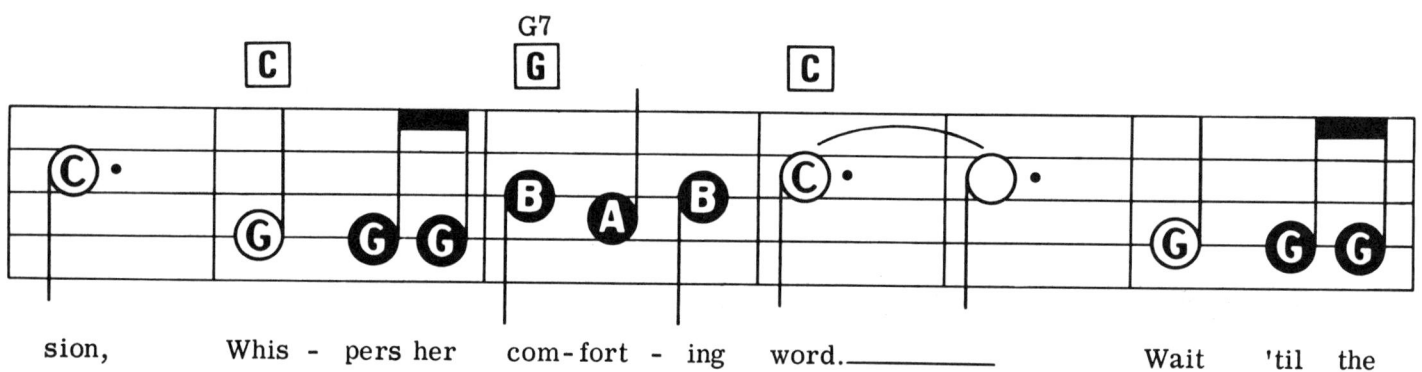
sion, Whis - pers her com - fort - ing word._____ Wait 'til the

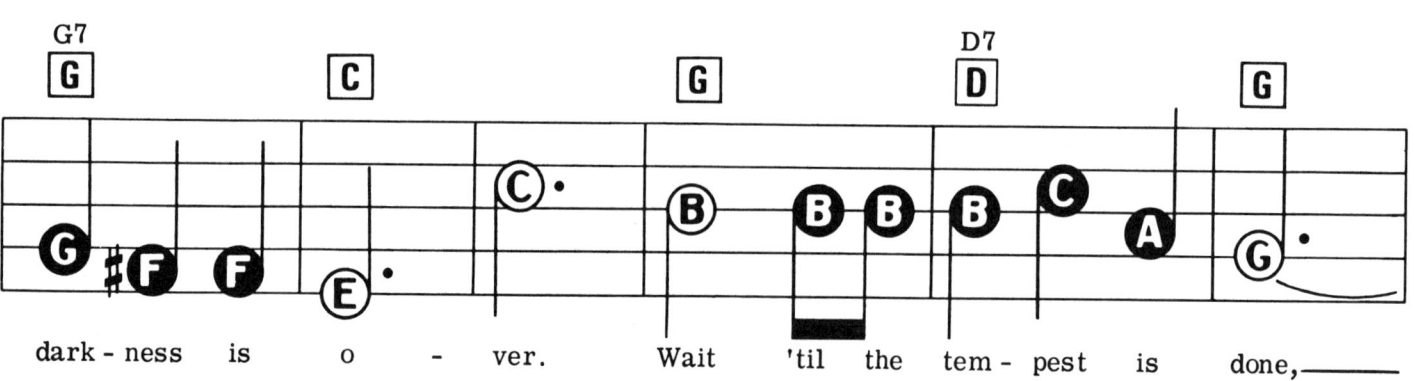
dark - ness is o - ver. Wait 'til the tem - pest is done,_____

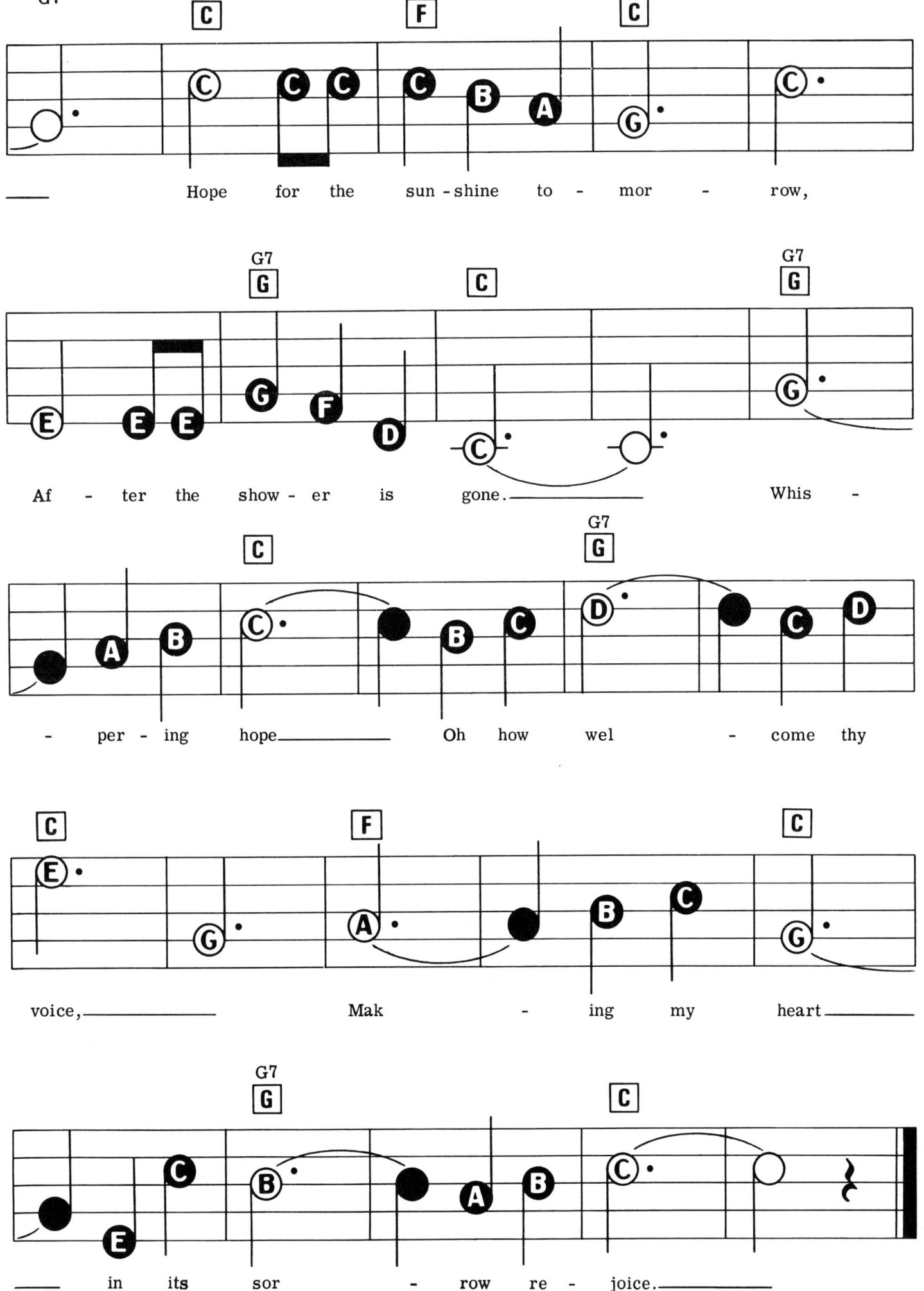

Praise God, From Whom All Blessings Flow